Education and the Human Rights Act 1998

Simon Whitbourn

Published in June 2003
by the National Foundation for Educational Research,
The Mere, Upton Park, Slough, Berkshire SL1 2DQ

ISBN 1 903880 46 7

Contents

Preface

To cynics, the Human Rights Act 1998 was, and will continue to be, a controversial piece of legislation: a source of anxiety and alarm for the tabloids; a source of much litigation and hence income for the lawyers.

At the time of its implementation in October 2000, the Act generated a great number of books, articles and training courses. Many were helpful and informative but many, unfortunately, were no more than attempts to leap onto what was seen as a potentially profitable band wagon.

The Human Rights Act was a significant step for United Kingdom law, but also a leap into the unknown. Consequently, whatever the intentions, much of the information written or presented at the time could be no more than guesswork: lawyers gazing into crystal balls. And although much was made of the potential impact of the 1998 Act on the world of education, no work specifically dedicated to this aspect of the Act was, to the author's knowledge, produced.

The AEC (Association of Education Committees) Trust and EMIE (Education Management Information Exchange) sought to rectify this gap. Sensibly they chose to wait until the Act had bedded down and the case law developed before commissioning this work. The fact that comparatively few education cases have been brought, and hence that publication has been delayed until it was possible to report on a number of key cases, is reassurance in itself that the impact of the Act has been less than predicted, a reassurance which, hopefully, this work will reinforce.

Human rights law can be complicated: not just in its substance, but in the way it has been incorporated into United Kingdom law and in the way it draws reference from jurisprudence and case law which is sometimes unfamiliar to United Kingdom practitioners. To deal with the latter, the table of abbreviations attempts to list the various law reports and periodicals cited throughout. As to the former, the Human Rights Act 1998 incorporates a number of the Articles set out in the European Convention on Human Rights into United Kingdom law. References throughout this book to Convention Rights or Articles are therefore, unless otherwise indicated, references to the European Convention Rights and Articles set out in Schedule 1 to the 1998 Act and which have been so incorporated into United Kingdom law.

Given the current state of development of this area of law, more opinion or, to put it more bluntly, informed guesswork is included within this work than is perhaps usual. I wish therefore to make clear that such expressions of opinion are those of the author and must not be imputed to the National Foundation for Educational Research, EMIE or the AEC Trust.

This work is intended to be informative and helpful and to provide a guide to the law as at 28 February 2003. It cannot purport, however, to provide legal guidance on particular issues or cases or offer any authoritative interpretation of the law. And, as always, responsibility for errors and omissions in the text remains with the author.

© Neil Bennett/Times Newspapers

Acknowledgements

The author wishes to thank the AEC (Association of Education Committees Trust) for providing a grant towards the production of this work and for awaiting the finished publication so patiently. The generosity of the Trustees is much appreciated. He is also grateful to all the unnamed education officers, particularly at Hampshire County Council, head teachers and governors with whom he has worked and been able to discuss the practical implications of the 1998 Act. Without their help many of the day to day effects set out in the book may well have been missed.

Special thanks go to Dr Robert Morris, lately Editor of the *Law of Education* Bulletin, for reading the draft of this book and offering his, as always, incisive and helpful comments and suggestions; and to Kenneth Poole, solicitor, and formerly an Editor of Butterworths' standard textbook, *The Law of Education*, for his advice and for kindly agreeing to review this guide.

We are indebted to Richard Downing for his contribution to the book, in particular the preparation of the table of statutes and the index, and to Janet May-Bowles, Head of the NFER's Library and Information Services for her help with this publication.

The assistance and guidance of other NFER colleagues, Mary Hargreaves, Media Resources Officer, Val Hincks, Media and Communications Manager, Alison Lawson, Editorial and Publishing Manager, and Wendy Tury, Head of Communications and Marketing, is gratefully acknowledged, as is the input of EMIE's Technical Officers, Kerry Hall and Alison Riley, and Senior Information Officers, Jo Richards and Monica Hetherington.

Finally, the author wishes to express his gratitude to Valerie Gee and Jeff Griffiths, Head and Deputy Head of EMIE, for organising and guiding this project.

About the Author

Simon Whitbourn is a solicitor specialising in education and public law. He was previously Principal Solicitor with Hampshire County Council, but now runs his own practice. His clients include the Department for Education and Skills, the English Tourist Council and a number of local education authorities and schools to whom he provides advice and training, especially on admissions, exclusions and the associated appeals.

Simon's previous books include *What is the LEA for? An Analysis of the Functions and Roles of the Local Education Authority* (EMIE/NFER) and *Special Educational Needs and Disability in Education: A Legal Guide* (Butterworths). He is a contributor to Butterworths' *Education Law Manual* and has written many articles for education and local government journals.

Table of Cases

Table of Statutes

Circulars

DfE Circular 7/87 Education (No 2) Act 1986:
Further Guidance — 8.5.2

DfES Circular 10/99 Social inclusion: pupil support — 8.7.10, 8.7.18, 8.7.22

DfES Circular 11/99 Social Exclusion:
the LEA Role in Pupil Support — 9.5

Guidance

DfEE 0016/2000
Admissions to infant classes from September 2000 — 6.5.4

DfES/0774/2001
Inclusive Schooling: Children with Special Educational Needs — 10.4.2

International legislation

Convention for the Protection of Human Rights
and Fundamental Freedoms 1950 preamble — 2.2.3

Art 2	4.1.3, 4.1.4, 4.2, 13.3.1, 13.4.5, 15.2.2
Art 3	4.1.3, 4.3, 7.5.6, 8.3.4, 8.6.5, 8.7.10, 13.3.1, 14.4.2, 14.4.3, 15.2.2
Art 4	4.1.3, 4.1.6, 4.4, 13.4.2, 13.4.3, 14.4.4
Art 5	4.5, 7.4.2, 7.4.3, 8.3.2, 8.3.3,15.2.2
Art 5(1)(d)	8.3.1,
Art 6	3.12.6, 4.1.6, 4.6, 6.2.15, 6.4.5, 7.2.12, 7.2.14, 8.7.5, 8.7.9, 8.7.19, 8.7.21, 8.7.26, 8.7.27, 8.7.28, 8.7.36, 8.7.37, 10.2.1, 10.5.2, 10.5.5, 10.5.10, 12.2.5, 14.5.1, 14.5.2, 15.5.1, 15.6.2
Art 6(1)	3.12.6
Art 6(2)	3.12.6
Art (3)	3.12.6
Art 7	4.7
Art 8	3.7.18, 4.8, 5.3.5, 6.3.6, 6.3.8, 7.2.18, 7.2.19, 7.2.20, 7.2.21, 7.2.22, 7.2.23, 7.2.24, 8.2.3, 9.12, 10.2.1, 10.3.2, 10.3.3, 10.3.4, 10.3.5, 10.3.7, 10.3.8, 10.4.4, 10.5.5, 11.3.1, 12.3.3, 13.3.1, 13.4.5, 13.4.6, 13.5.3, 14.3.1, 14.3.2, 14.3.3
Art 8(2)	4.8.3, 4.8.6, 4.8.11, 10.3.6, 13.5.3
Art 9	4.9, 4.10.2, 5.3.5, 7.2.6, 7.2.7, 7.5.4, 14.2.5, 14.2.6
Art 10	3.7.10, 4.10, 8.5.1, 8.5.3, 8.5.4, 8.5.7, 8.5.8, 8.7.12, 8.7.14, 11.3.1, 14.2.1, 14.2.4
Art 11	4.11, 7.4.2
Art 12	4.1.6, 4.12, 11.3.1
Art 13.	2.3.3

1. Introduction

1.1 In October 2000, the Human Rights Act 1998 was brought into force to a fanfare of gloom, panic and pessimism among certain sections of the media: '*Human rights "free for all" feared*' [*Daily Telegraph*, 7 August 2000], '*Scare stories and jitters in Whitehall*' [*Daily Telegraph*, 7 August 2000] and '*Citizen Straw and his politicos will find this a hard Act to follow*' [*The Independent*, 1 October 2000].

1.2 The '*Scare stories and jitters in Whitehall*' was particularly typical of the alarms being sounded that the introduction of the Act would bring public authorities to their knees with every dissatisfied citizen taking them to the courts over every insignificant matter: 'as "Human Rights Day" approaches, there are signs of concern in Whitehall and Westminster about the potential impact of the legislation – and Tony Blair has refused an invitation to speak at the launch. David Lidington, the Tory home affairs spokesman, said last night that he believed there would be a "torrent of litigation". The police were already saying that professional criminals were preparing to use human rights defences as a matter of course.' The experience of Scotland, which had incorporated the European Convention on Human Rights one year earlier, did not bode too well either as, by some means known only to the Scottish High Court, they contrived to allow Convention Rights to throw their entire criminal justice system into limbo [*Starrs and Chalmers v Procurator Fiscal* [1999] ScotHC 242 – a decision of the Scottish High Court which held that the use of Deputy Sheriffs appointed on an annual basis by the executive was unlawful].

1.3 Law firms geared up to provide advice on the implications of the Human Rights Act and barristers moved chambers in an attempt to set themselves up as the leading practitioners in the Human Rights field. Even the Home Office, the Department responsible for the Act becoming law, proudly stated that 'Human Rights were coming home'.

What has happened since then?

1.4 It is true that a number of cases have been brought and, as expected, challenges have been made to decisions relating to immigration, the criminal justice process, mental health and the prison service. For a while there was confusion over the entire planning appeal process but in reality civilisation has not broken down and the army of lawyers have not yet battered their way through the town hall doors. Occasional cases have continued to receive publicity: the odd nudist or two has shinned up a lamppost outside the Royal Courts of Justice and proclaimed their freedom to wave their bits about in public view [see, for example, '*Nudist campaigner walks from court a free (and naked) man'* [*Independent*, 11 January 2001]; and the occasional prisoner serving a life sentence has attempted to use the 1998 Act to gain freedom from censorship of his post, conjugal visits from his partner and, in one case, the right to take annual holidays and nip off for two weeks down to Benidorm [see *'Murderer claims the minimum wage and jail holidays under the new Act', The Independent*, 18 October 2000]. All of which have, needless to say, prompted tabloid outrage.

1.5   But in reality, two years on, the Human Rights Act appears to have settled down far more sensibly than anyone predicted. Comparisons with the millennium bug and its impact (or rather lack of it) are not very wide of the mark.

1.6   The European Convention on Human Rights, which the Human Rights Act incorporates directly into UK law, was designed to protect fundamental human rights, not the trivial. And it is quite right that the courts have recognised that the Act should not be used to bring vexatious challenges in respect of the irrelevant, the insignificant or downright disingenuous use of its provisions.

1.7   This has been particularly true in the education field where alarm bells were again sounded that schools and local education authorities would be fettered in the way that they could deal with pupils, parents and their employees. Probably all LEAs can cite cases of parents or pupils claiming that their human rights had been infringed [for reasons of lawyer/client confidentiality and the laws of libel the source of this anecdote cannot be named but the prize for the first example of the invocation of the 1998 Act allegedly went to a secondary school which had refused to admit a child. The child in question had semi-permanently tattooed the word 'Thug' across his forehead (although in reality, as he had done the tattoo in a mirror, it actually said 'GUHT'). It is understood that no claim was subsequently brought] but no significant claims have been made and some of the processes which were initially considered susceptible to challenge, such as independent admission and exclusion appeal panels, have been held to be human rights compliant by the courts [see Chapters 6 and 8].

1.8   A further reason for the lack of litigation has most probably been the pre-existing compliance of much of the domestic law with the Convention even before the Human Rights Act was enacted. This has been due partly to domestic concepts of administrative law, natural justice, fair hearing etc., but also to the fact that areas where the law had not been compliant with the Convention had already been tested in the European Court of Human Rights and reformed as a consequence [for example, the abolition of corporal punishment after the cases of *Campbell and Cosans v United Kingdom* (1982) Series A No 48, 4 EHRR 293 and *Costello-Roberts v United Kingdom* (1993) Series A No 247-C, 19 EHRR 112].

1.9   In this context much has been made of the UK's previous bad 'form' in front of the European Court and it is true that it does not have the best of records. But to put the cases against the UK into context, in 2001 there were 474 applications registered against the UK in the ECtHR. This, though, pales into insignificance when compared to Italy's 590 (down from 882 in 1999) and France's 1,117. Even those figures cannot compare with the applications received against countries in Eastern Europe which have only recently submitted themselves to the jurisdiction of the ECtHR; Rumania 542, Poland 1,763 and, perhaps not surprisingly, Russia topping the league with 2,108 applications registered against it.

1.10   One thing which has kept UK lawyers busy and legal publishers in lives of luxury is the fact that the Human Rights Act has, in effect, imported European Convention case law as well as the Convention itself into UK law. Although Strasbourg precedent is not binding, it does have to be taken into account and it is therefore important to have a knowledge of the most important and relevant cases. [A factor which can be annoying and may become evident as the reader works through this book is that the Commission and ECtHR are keen to provide anonymity to claimants, especially where minors are involved, usually by substituting X for the party's name. This unfortunately can lead to some confusion as, for example, there are at least 12 cases cited as '*X v United Kingdom*' and at least another 20 '*X's*' involving other countries.]

1.11   This book attempts to provide an analysis of this case law and apply it to various aspects of education law. By waiting for more than two years after the Human Rights Act came into force, it is, hopefully, also able to refer to domestic case law (both English and Welsh or Scots) in an attempt to identify aspects of the law which are at risk under the Human Rights Act or where potential challenges may appear. The problem, though it is probably only a problem for lawyers, not for those who have to work in schools and LEAs, is that there have been so few cases and vast tracts of education law have still not been tested to see if, to coin one of many buzz phrases resulting from the 1998 Act, they are Human Rights Act compliant.

1.12   Indeed, when this book was commissioned, the hope was that it would be able to rely on hard and fast case law and experience so as to put it at an advantage over the earlier works on the 1998 Act's effect, which had, in many cases, been no more than attempts to peer into a rather murky, legal crystal ball. Sadly, though, this means that due to the absence of so many forecast cases a lot of this work still remains speculative and the personal opinion, some would say guesswork, of the author as to how the Human Rights Act will affect the world of LEAs and schools in the future.

1.13 The benefit of the absence of judicial activity, is, however, that books produced this long after the Act's implementation, should, to a certain extent, be works of reassurance, not alarm, as some of the earlier works may have been. There is no doubt that the Human Rights Act deals with fundamental and important rights; at times, the most fundamental rights of all, the rights to life and liberty. The press sniping and criticisms should not detract from its role in dealing with some of the most significant issues of our time for example, the separation of Siamese twins [*A (Children)* [2000] EWCA Civ 254], the right to conceive [*R v Human Fertilisation and Embryology Authority ex parte DB* [1997] EWCA Civ 946] or the right to decide whether to live itself [*Pretty v. Director of Public Prosecutions and Secretary of State for the Home Department* [2001] UKHL 61 and, in the ECtHR, *Pretty v United Kingdom* Application 2346/02, 29 April 2002].

1.14 Do not therefore belittle the Human Rights Act simply because it throws up the occasional odd ball or the unbelievable example of a lawyer willing to chance their arm in the face of all logic. Remember instead what the Act, or rather the Convention before it, was designed to achieve: the protection of human rights and fundamental freedoms – and perhaps be grateful.

1.15 The Human Rights Act will not force the rights of an individual to triumph over the interests of society in general; as will be seen, most Articles in the Convention involve a careful balancing act to ensure that a proper perspective is kept and that the rights of the eloquent and/or demanding few do not usurp those of others. In some ways it is unfortunate that it was not called the Human Rights and Responsibilities Act as all too often the responsibilities which go with the assertion of rights are forgotten. Nonetheless, the Act does recognise that the interest of society will frequently mean that an individual's claim will not succeed and this has been evident from the domestic case law to date.

1.16 For those of you working in education, there is a need for you to be aware of the Human Rights Act and its effects, recognise when human rights issues may arise, know when to take advice and, in certain cases, be prepared for challenge. Hopefully, though, the overall message of this book should be a cross between advice proffered by Lord Baden-Powell to his scouts and Corporal Jones to Captain Mainwaring:

Be Prepared but Don't Panic.

2. A Brief History of the European Convention on Human Rights and the Human Rights Act 1998

2.1 General overview

2.1.1 The Human Rights Act did not introduce new law as such into the UK. Nor did it introduce new protections for UK citizens. Since the UK Government ratified the European Convention in 1950, UK citizens had always enjoyed the protections of the Convention Rights. Initially, however, there was no right for individuals to petition the European Commission or Court direct. It was only at the beginning of 1966 that this means of redress was accepted by the UK Government.

2.1.2 But, even then, the right to individual petition was to the Commission or the Court; not to domestic courts or tribunals. If they wished to enforce their Convention Rights, UK citizens had to mount a challenge, in effect under international law, against the UK Government to the European Court in Strasbourg. Challenges against individual public authorities were therefore not possible, although a challenge could be mounted against the UK Government to attack the legislation which permitted individual authorities to behave in breach of Convention Rights.

2.1.3 Initially, the Convention had been little used by litigants. There had been only two cases between 1950 and 1966. Offering the right to petition did, however, provide a significant impetus for claims from within the UK and between 1966 and 1998 the Convention, as interpreted by the European Commission ('the Commission') and European Court of Human Rights ('the ECtHR'), had a significant impact on constitutional and public law within the UK.

2.1.4 The Human Rights Act principally, therefore, changes this situation by incorporating the Convention Rights directly into UK law and by giving an aggrieved individual ('a victim') the ability to enforce his or her Convention Rights in the UK courts. *Bringing Rights Home* was the message from the Government and *Rights Brought Home: The Human Rights Bill* the title of the White Paper which preceded the Human Rights Act. The 1998 Act was seen by the Government as giving 'people in the United Kingdom opportunities to enforce their rights under the European Convention in British courts rather than having to incur the cost and delay of taking a case to the European Human Rights... Court in Strasbourg.' [Preface to *Rights Brought Home: The Human Rights Bill*]

2.1.5 The emphasis on bringing rights home was important because of the nature of the Convention as an international treaty. As such, as a matter of English law, provision in a treaty could not be part of domestic law unless and until it has been incorporated into UK law by legislation [see, for example, *JH Rayner (Mincing Lane) Ltd v Department of Trade and Industry* [1990] 2 AC 418, per Lord Oliver at p500]. As will be seen below [see 2.2.1*ff*], the Convention had not been ignored, but its effect was limited and it could not bestow substantive rights on UK citizens.

2.1.6 In a number of important cases in the domestic courts, the Convention had been raised but its usefulness was generally limited to being a means of assisting in the interpretation of UK law. Thus, it was used to resolve ambiguity if a statute subsequent to the Convention affecting a person's Convention Rights was at odds with the Convention [see, for example, *R v Secretary of State for the Home Department ex p Brind* [1991] 1 AC 696]. In other cases, the courts would turn to the Convention if they had to apply the common law but found it unclear [see, for example, *AG v Guardian Newspapers Ltd (No 2)* [1990] 1 AC 109]. The courts also accepted that where a case involving a public authority against an individual concerned liberties or freedoms which were of the sort protected by the Convention, that justified greater judicial scrutiny of a public authority's exercise of discretion [see *R v Ministry of Defence ex p Smith* [1996] QB 57, CA].

2.1.7 Nonetheless, the UK courts were always having to tiptoe around the fact that they could not directly apply Convention rights; there was inconsistency in approach between judges and the search for ambiguity in order to invoke the Convention as an aid to interpretation could lead to uncertainty in litigation.

2.1.8 By introducing the Human Rights Bill therefore, the Government took the necessary steps to incorporate Convention Rights directly into English law (the Convention was incorporated into Scottish law through the Scotland Act 1998 and, in Wales, through the Government of Wales Act 1998, insofar as this Act required the National Assembly for Wales to ensure that its subordinate legislation and other actions were Convention Compliant) and enable English courts and tribunals to apply directly the rights and principles which until then had been the preserve of their judicial colleagues across the Channel in Strasbourg.

2.2 Use by English courts of the Convention up to 2000

2.2.1 As stated, 'European Convention Law', as it may be known, was not a new concept. The European Convention itself was produced in 1950 and ratified by the UK Government in 1951. Ironically, given the delay in its incorporation into domestic law, the Convention was driven by the then UK Government and, despite, as we shall see, the 'European' method of construction and interpretation applied by the ECtHR, British civil servants played a key role in its drafting.

2.2.2 It was, however, a creature of its time; a response to the abuses of human rights perpetrated before, during and immediately after the Second World War and a recognition of the need to protect the individual against totalitarian Government in whatever guise. And it was designed to address *fundamental* abuses – an important factor to bear in mind when considering how the *fundamental* Convention Rights should be applied in the domestic, and particularly the educational, setting.

2.2.3 The Preamble to the Convention illustrates the emphasis that the signatories placed on these fundamental rights and freedoms:

> 'The Governments signatory hereto, being Members of the Council of Europe,
>
> Considering the Universal Declaration of Human Rights proclaimed by the General Assembly of the United Nations on 10 December 1948;
>
> Considering that this Declaration aims at securing the universal and effective recognition and observance of the Rights therein declared;
>
> Considering that the aim of the Council of Europe is the achievement of greater unity between its members and that one of the methods by which the aim is to be pursued is the maintenance and further realization of human rights and fundamental freedoms;
>
> Reaffirming their profound belief in those fundamental freedoms which are the foundation of justice and peace in the world and are best maintained on the one hand by an effective political democracy and on the other by a common understanding and observance of the human rights upon which they depend;
>
> Being resolved, as the Governments of European countries which are like-minded and have a common heritage of political traditions, ideals, freedom and the rule of law to take the first steps for the collective enforcement of certain of the rights stated in the Universal Declaration
>
> Have agreed as follows:'

2.2.4 The Convention was based significantly on the United Nations Universal Declaration of Human Rights of 1948. That Declaration's Preamble also reflected the time and circumstances in which it was drafted:

> 'Whereas recognition of the inherent dignity and the equal and inalienable rights of all members of the human family is the foundation of freedom, justice and peace in the world;

> Whereas disregard and contempt for human rights have resulted in barbarous acts which have outraged the conscience of mankind, and the advent of a world in which human beings shall enjoy freedom of speech and belief and freedom from fear and want has been proclaimed as the highest aspiration of the common people.'

2.2.5 The aim of the Convention was thus to protect the fundamental freedoms of individuals within the territories of signatory states and to provide a minimum safeguard against the abuse of state power.

2.2.6 As a child of its time, however, the Convention was aimed at preventing a repetition of the Holocaust, of show trials, forced labour and state sanctioned execution. It did not therefore initially address certain other rights which might be considered as fundamental human rights, the right to education being one example. Consequently, Protocols to the Convention have been produced and ratified by some of the original signatories in an attempt to cover these original omissions. The Convention, nonetheless, remains a mechanism for protecting an individual from state abuse; it does not guarantee economic or social welfare rights.

2.2.7 Having been one of the first to ratify the Convention, it is well known that the UK Government declined to incorporate the Convention Rights into UK law for 47 years, leaving it simply as a matter of international law with aggrieved individuals having to bring their complaint against the Government to the ECtHR, although even that right to petition was only grudgingly and belatedly granted. English courts had occasionally referred to the Government's Convention obligations in interpreting certain provisions of UK law but, in principle, no citizen could seek a remedy for a public body's breach of their Convention Rights in a UK court or tribunal.

2.2.8 In 1997 a new Labour Government was elected with a commitment to incorporate the Convention directly into UK law by way of the necessary Acts of Parliament. In Scotland and Wales the opportunity was taken to incorporate the Convention through the devolution legislation [see the Scotland Act 1998 and the Government of Wales Act 1998] and the Human Rights Act 1998. In England, however, the mechanism was solely the Human Rights Act 1998.

2.3 How the Human Rights Act incorporates the European Convention

2.3.1 The key to the Human Rights Act is that it incorporates rights established under the European Convention directly into UK law. As stated, this means that an aggrieved individual can seek redress from national courts or tribunals or raise human rights points in domestic proceedings, rather than have to take a case to the ECtHR in Strasbourg as was the situation before the coming into force of the Act.

2.3.2 In practice, this should provide a speedier and more economic means of redress and will mean that the European Convention is considered as part of national UK law, rather than being a creature of international law.

2.3.3 The Human Rights Act does not, however, incorporate all the rights contained in the European Convention and its protocols. Those that have not been incorporated remain binding on the UK Government (other than those to which derogations have been obtained) but as rights in international, not national, law. They therefore cannot be enforced against public bodies below Governmental level. Such rights include: the right to an effective remedy (Article 13); prohibition of imprisonment for debt (Article 1 of the Fourth Protocol) and the prohibition of collective expulsion of aliens (Article 4 of the Fourth Protocol).

3. The Fundamental Principles of the Human Rights Act

3.1 Introduction

3.1.1   This chapter will outline some of the general principles of the law relating to the European Convention and how it is to be applied into UK law through the Human Rights Act.

3.2 Legislation to be read to give effect to Convention Rights

3.2.1   So far as it is possible to do so, primary legislation and subordinate legislation must be read and given effect in a way which is compatible with rights guaranteed under the Convention [s 3 Human Rights Act].

3.2.2   An important facet of 'reading' the Act is how courts, tribunals and public authorities should interpret its provisions. This is where the Human Rights Act and the Convention has brought about a sea change in English law. The English system of precedent and interpretation has generally been seen as one of strict application. Although the courts in recent years have been more prepared to depart from a strict towards a purposive interpretation of primary and subordinate legislation, the principle has generally been one of strict adherence to the letter and wording of the law.

3.2.3   In contrast, different principles of interpretation apply in the jurisprudence of the European Court and in their interpretation of the Convention. This is primarily because the provisions of an enactment giving effect to basic freedoms 'call for a generous interpretation avoiding what has been called the "austerity of tabulated legalism", suitable to give individuals the full measure of the fundamental rights and freedoms referred to' [*Ministry of Home Affairs v Fisher* [1980] AC 319, per Lord Wilberforce].

3.2.4   As the Convention is an international treaty, the principles of interpretation set out in the Vienna Convention on the Law of Treaties will apply. Thus, a treaty must be interpreted in good faith, by reference both to its wording and to its object and purpose and having regard to subsequent practice [Vienna Convention on the Law of Treaties Articles 31 to 33]. But, even here, the European Convention is an atypical treaty vesting rights in individuals rather than regulating the affairs of states. Even greater weight than usual has therefore been given to its object and purpose and attempts to apply a narrow construction have been rejected [see, for example, *Wemhoff v Germany* (1968) Ser. A. No 7; 1 EHRR 55]. Instead, the Commission has stated in *Loizidou v Turkey* [(1995) Ser A, No 310, 20 EHRR 99] that 'the object and purpose of the Convention as an instrument for the protection of individual human beings require that its provisions be interpreted so as to make its safeguards practical and effective'. A re-emphasis, in effect, of the fact that courts and tribunals should apply a purposive interpretation, looking at the object of the protection bestowed rather than carrying out a precise, literal examination of its wording.

3.
FUNDAMENTAL
PRINCIPLES

3.2.5   An important point though is the reference in the Vienna Convention to having regard to subsequent practice. This means that interpretation of the Convention Rights should evolve to reflect the context in which the Right is being considered: the Convention is therefore 'a living instrument which must be interpreted in the light of present-day conditions' [see *Loizidou v Turkey,* supra and *Tyrer v United Kingdom* (1978) 2 EHRR 1 at p 10]. Assistance in the interpretation cannot therefore always be obtained from the *travaux préparatoires,* which accompanied the original Convention [the Convention 'cannot be interpreted solely in accordance with the intention of its authors as expressed more than 40 years ago', *Loizidou v Turkey*], nor from previous decisions of either the Commission or ECtHR or, for that matter, UK courts. The familiar English doctrine of precedent therefore has only a limited place in human rights law. This is particularly important where society's attitudes have changed over time and where, as a consequence, earlier judgments from different times may not always be relied upon, an example, being the changing attitude towards sexual orientation and the notion of family.

3.2.6   Discussion of the use of precedent brings us on to two related topics: the institutions established by the Convention and the status of their decisions when UK courts come to decide human rights claims.

3.3   The organs of the European Convention

3.3.1   In addition to laying down civil and political rights and freedoms, the Convention set up a system of enforcement originally comprising three institutions: the European Commission of Human Rights (set up in 1954) ('the Commission'), the European Court of Human Rights (set up in 1959) ('the ECtHR') and the Committee of Ministers of the Council of Europe, the last being composed of the Ministers for Foreign Affairs of the member States or their representatives ('the Committee of Ministers').

3.3.2 Under the 1950 Convention Contracting States and, where the Contracting States had accepted the right of individual petition, individual applicants (individuals, groups of individuals or non-Governmental organisations) could lodge complaints against Contracting States for alleged violations of Convention Rights.

3.3.3 The complaints were first the subject of a preliminary examination by the Commission, which determined their admissibility. Where applications had been declared admissible and no friendly settlement had been reached, the Commission drew up a report establishing the facts and expressing an opinion on the merits of the case. The report was transmitted to the Committee of Ministers.

3.3.4 Where the respondent State had accepted the compulsory jurisdiction of the ECtHR, the Commission and/or any Contracting State concerned had a period of three months following the transmission of the report to the Committee of Ministers within which to bring the case before the ECtHR for a final, binding adjudication. Individuals were not entitled to bring their cases before the ECtHR.

3.3.5 If a case was not referred to the ECtHR, the Committee of Ministers decided whether there had been a violation of the Convention and, if appropriate, awarded just satisfaction to the victim. The Committee of Ministers also had responsibility for supervising the execution of the ECtHR's judgments.

3.3.6 As seemingly with all courts, the growth in litigation under the Convention led to significant delays in the system, especially as the number of Contracting States grew in the 1990s with the accession of countries from Eastern Europe. The number of applications registered annually with the Commission increased from 404 in 1981 to 4,750 in 1997. By 1997 the number of unregistered or provisional files opened each year in the Commission had risen to over 12,000. The ECtHR faced a similar problem with the number of cases referred annually rising from 7 in 1981 to 52 in 1993 and 119 in 1997. The increase in cases led to a review of the mechanisms, with the result that the role of the Commission was abolished, the Committee of Ministers lost its adjudicative role and the ECtHR was re-established as a single, full-time court.

3.3.7 The new European Court of Human Rights came into operation on 1 November 1998 with the entry into force of Protocol No. 11. On 31 October 1998, the old Court had ceased to function. However, the Protocol provided that the Commission should continue for one year (until 31 October 1999) to deal with cases which had been declared admissible before the date of entry into force of the Protocol.

3.3.8   The ECtHR as now established is composed of a number of judges equal to that of the Contracting States (currently forty one). Judges are elected by the Parliamentary Assembly of the Council of Europe for a term of six years. Judges sit on the Court in their individual capacity and do not represent any State. Under the Rules of Court, the Court is divided into four Sections, whose composition, fixed for three years, is geographically and gender balanced and takes account of the different legal systems of the Contracting States. Each Section is presided over by a President, two of the Section Presidents being at the same time Vice-Presidents of the Court. Section Presidents are assisted and, where necessary, replaced by Section Vice-Presidents.

3.3.9   Committees of three judges are set up within each Section for periods of twelve months and Chambers of seven members are constituted within each Section on the basis of rotation, with the Section President and the judge elected in respect of the State concerned sitting in each case. Where the latter is not a member of the Section, he or she sits as an *ex officio* member of the Chamber. The members of the Section who are not full members of the Chamber sit as substitute members.

3.3.10   The Grand Chamber is composed of seventeen judges. The President, Vice-Presidents, Section Presidents and the judge elected in respect of the State concerned sit as *ex officio* members. The remaining judges are chosen by the drawing of lots.

3.3.11   The procedure before the ECtHR is adversarial and public unless the Chamber/Grand Chamber decides otherwise on account of exceptional circumstances.

3.3.12   Each application is assigned to a Section, whose President designates a rapporteur. After a preliminary examination of the case, the rapporteur decides whether it should be dealt with by a three-member Committee or by a Chamber. A Committee may decide, by unanimous vote, to declare inadmissible or strike out an application where it can do so without further examination. Applications which are not declared inadmissible by Committees or which are referred directly to a Chamber by the rapporteur and State applications are examined by a Chamber. Chambers determine both admissibility and merits, usually in separate decisions but where appropriate together.

3.3.13   Chambers may at any time relinquish jurisdiction in favour of the Grand Chamber where a case raises a serious question of interpretation of the Convention or where there is a risk of departing from existing case law, unless one of the parties objects to such relinquishment within one month of notification of the intention to relinquish.

3.3.14 The first stage of the procedure is generally written, although the Chamber may decide to hold a hearing, in which case issues arising in relation to the merits will normally also be addressed. Once the Chamber has decided to admit the application, it may invite the parties to submit further evidence and written observations, including any claims for 'just satisfaction' by the applicant, and to attend a public hearing on the merits of the case. The President of the Chamber may, in the interests of the proper administration of justice, invite or grant leave to any Contracting State which is not party to the proceedings, or any person concerned who is not the applicant, to submit written comments, and, in exceptional circumstances, to make representations at the hearing. A Contracting State whose national is an applicant in the case is entitled to intervene as of right.

3.3.15 Chambers decide by a majority vote. Any judge who has taken part in the consideration of the case is entitled to append to the judgment a separate opinion, either concurring or dissenting, or a bare statement of dissent. Within three months of delivery of the judgment by a Chamber, any party may request that the case be referred to the Grand Chamber if it raises a serious question of interpretation or application or a serious issue of general importance. Such requests are examined by a Grand Chamber panel of five judges composed of the President of the Court, the Section Presidents and another judge. If the panel accepts the request, the Grand Chamber renders its decision on the case in the form of a judgment. The Grand Chamber decides by a majority vote and its judgments are final.

3.3.16 A Chamber's judgment becomes final at the expiry of the three-month period or earlier if the parties announce that they have no intention of requesting a referral or after a decision of the panel rejecting the request for referral.

3.3.17 All final judgments of the ECtHR are binding on the respondent States concerned. Responsibility for supervising the execution of judgments lies with the Committee of Ministers. One of the roles of the Committee of Ministers is therefore to verify whether States found to be in breach of the Convention have taken adequate remedial measures to comply with the ECtHR's judgment.

3.3.18 The ECtHR may, at the request of the Committee of Ministers, provide advisory opinions on legal questions concerning the interpretation of the Convention and its Protocols. Such opinions are given by the Grand Chamber.

3.3.19 The case load is nonetheless still increasing and review continues in an attempt to eliminate cases which are vexatious or raise no significant Convention point.

3.4 Effect of Strasbourg jurisprudence in United Kingdom law

3.4.1 Opinions and decision from the two 'old' organs as well as the new single court must be taken into account by English courts and tribunals, thus opening up a market for human rights law reports and a rush amongst lawyers in October 2000 to catch up on at least 40 years of potentially relevant case law.

3.4.2 A court or tribunal when determining a question which has arisen in connection with a Convention Right must take into account any:

(a) judgment, decision, declaration or advisory opinion of the ECtHR;

(b) opinion of the Commission given in a report adopted under Article 31 of the Convention (i.e. reports by the Commission on the merits of a case after they have been declared admissible; from 1 November 1999, these will no longer be produced);

(c) decision of the Commission in connection with Article 26 or 27(2) of the Convention (i.e. admissibility decisions; again, from 1 November 1999, these will no longer be produced); or

(d) decision of the Committee of Ministers taken under Article 46 of the Convention (i.e. reports prepared by the Committee of Ministers in its role as supervisor of the execution of ECtHR judgments); whenever made or given, so far as it is relevant to the proceedings [s 2(1) Human Rights Act].

3.4.3 Although not expressed as such, in effect, s 2(1) of the Human Rights Act lays down a hierarchy of precedent and, in the event of any conflict, a judgment or decision higher up the list will take priority. These decisions or judgments must be taken into account; but courts and tribunals are therefore not bound to follow them. Under normal principles, they should do, but where there are good reasons, it is permissible for a departure from the precedent (for example, because it is an old decision and society has changed) to occur.

3.4.4 Of course, in addition to the European case law, UK courts and tribunals will also be required (as and when the case law develops) to take account of domestic precedent. There , however, be a slight deviation from the normal rules of precedent to the extent that the dynamic, evolving interpretation may be applied to reflect judicial understanding of changes in society.

3.5   No power to strike down primary legislation

3.5.1   Where it is not possible to read other legislation compatibly with Convention Rights, the Human Rights Act confers no power on the court or tribunal to strike down such legislation. Despite concerns expressed to the contrary during the Act's passage through Parliament, the Act is therefore subject to the sovereignty of Parliament. It is possible for Parliament to introduce primary legislation or to keep in place legislation which is or continues to be incompatible with the Human Rights Act. It is conceivable therefore that subsequent legislation could repeal the Human Rights Act; it is not entrenched in the same way as bills of rights are in other jurisdictions.

3.6   The powers of United Kingdom courts

3.6.1   Having said that, however, the Human Rights Act does provide the judiciary with a wider opportunity to enter into the realms of social and political comment, because there are powers under the Act, first, for the courts to strive to give effect to legislation in a way which is compatible with the Convention, second, for courts and tribunals to strike down subordinate legislation which is incompatible with the Act and, third, for the higher courts to issue declarations of incompatibility.

Reading of legislation

3.6.2   As considered above, s 3 of the Human Rights Act regulates the interrelationship between domestic legislation and the Convention. 'So far as it is possible to do so, primary legislation and subordinate legislation must be read and given effect in a way which is compatible with the Convention Rights.' [s 3(1) Human Rights Act] This applies to primary and subordinate legislation, whenever enacted [although, for a consideration of the retrospective effect of the Human Rights Act see 3.9.2*ff* below], but does not affect either the validity, continuing operation or enforcement of any incompatible primary legislation nor the validity, continuing operation or enforcement of any incompatible subordinate legislation if (disregarding the possibility of revocation) primary legislation prevents removal of the incompatibility [s 3(2) Human Rights Act].

Striking down subordinate legislation and declarations of incompatibility

3.6.3   Striking down subordinate legislation is not new; it has been a feature of administrative law for years for courts to quash delegated legislation. Declarations of incompatibility are, on the other hand, an innovation and it will be interesting to see how the courts (and it is courts, these declarations can be made only by the High Court, Court of Appeal or House of Lords) develop their use.

3.6.4   As mentioned above, Parliamentary Sovereignty is preserved so far as primary legislation is concerned. If a higher court considers that primary legislation is in breach of the Convention, it cannot strike that provision down. Instead, if the court is satisfied that the provision is incompatible with a Convention right, it may make a declaration of that incompatibility — 'a declaration of incompatibility' [s 4(2) Human Rights Act].

3.6.5   Similarly, if a higher court considers that a piece of subordinate legislation is incompatible, but the primary legislation under which it is made prevents the removal of that incompatibility (short of revoking the primary legislation), the court can also issue a similar declaration.

3.6.6   In either case, however, the issuing of a declaration does not affect the validity, continuing operation or enforcement of the provision in respect of which it was given [s 4(6)(b) Human Rights Act]. The declaration does not either have any effect on the parties to the action in which the declaration is made; the declaration is not binding on them [s 4(6)(b) Human Rights Act]. In effect, a declaration of incompatibility is little more than a note from the court to the Government drawing attention to a provision which the court sees as incompatible with Convention Rights.

3.6.7   Although hopefully unlikely, the Government need not respond to the declaration and could, in principle, simply ignore it. If, however, the Government acknowledges the appropriateness of the declaration, the Human Rights Act provides a speedy mechanism to secure amendment to the legislation, without the need to take amending primary legislation through Parliament [see s 10 Human Rights Act].

3.6.8   Thus, where a provision of legislation has been declared incompatible with a Convention right and if there is no further appeal, the relevant Minister of the Crown may take remedial action [s 10(1)(a) Human Rights Act]. That action is also available where it appears to a Minister of the Crown or Her Majesty in Council that, having regard to a finding of the ECtHR after the coming into force of s 10 of the Human Rights Act (i.e. 1 October 2000) in proceedings against the UK, a provision of legislation is incompatible with an obligation of the UK arising from the Convention [s 10(1)(b) Human Rights Act].

3.6.9   In either of these cases, if a Minister of the Crown believes that there are compelling reasons for proceeding, he or she may by order exercisable by statutory instrument [s 20(1) Human Rights Act] make such amendments to the legislation as he or she considers necessary to remove the incompatibility [s 10(2) Human Rights Act and see Schedule 2 Human Rights Act for the procedure for making a remedial order]. Use of such declarations has been rare and none have been made in the education field [for examples of their use elsewhere see, for example, *International Transport Roth GmbH and Others v Secretary of State for the Home Department* [2002] EWCA Civ 158 and *R v Mental Health Review Tribunal, North East London Region and Secretary of State for Health ex p H* [2001] EWCA Civ 415]. A Minister has similar power in relation to incompatible subordinate legislation to amend the primary legislation under which it is made to enable the incompatibility to be removed [s 10(3) Human Rights Act].

3.6.10   To avoid the problem of the Government being faced with a declaration of incompatibility in cases to which it is not party or has not received notice, s 5 provides the Crown with the right to intervene in any proceedings where the court is considering making a declaration of incompatibility. Thus where a court is considering making such a declaration, the Crown is entitled to notice; this may mean that in those cases to which the Crown is not already a party, the matter should be adjourned to allow the Crown to apply for the appropriate Minister to be joined as a party [s 5(2) Human Rights Act].

3.7   The duty imposed on public authorities to act compatibly with a person's Convention Rights

3.7.1   Underlying the whole structure of the Human Rights Act is the duty imposed on public authorities to act in a manner compatible with Convention Rights [s 6(1) Human Rights Acts].

3.7.2   The relevant Convention Rights are those set out in Schedule 1 to the 1998 Act which will be considered briefly below [see Chapters 4 and 5]. Those are comparatively straightforward. Where the principal difficulties were foreseen, and have been encountered, with this duty was the definition of 'a public authority'.

What are public authorities?

3.7.3   The Human Rights Act provides some assistance on who or what is a public authority, although not much. A 'public authority', we are told [s 6 (3) Human Rights Act], 'includes (a) a court or tribunal and (b) any person certain of whose functions are functions of a public nature, but does not include either House of Parliament or a person exercising functions in connections with proceedings in Parliament'. 'Parliament' here does not, however, include the House of Lords acting in its judicial capacity [s 6(4) Human Rights Act]. In addition, in relation to a particular act, a person is not a public authority (when otherwise they might be a public authority under s 6(3)(b) by virtue of having functions certain of which are of a public nature) if the nature of the act is private [s 6(5) Human Rights Act].

3.7.4   This definition is not easy – Jack Straw, the then Home Secretary, said that 'the matter is extremely complicated' [314 HC Official Report (6th Series) cols 408 –409] – but is important, especially in the context of an area such as education where pupils for whom LEAs are responsible can be placed in the non-maintained sector or where under the Private Finance Initiative (PFI), Public Private Partnership (PPP) or other forms of intervention, the distinction between public body and private company performing public functions is becoming increasingly blurred.

3.7.5   The Home Secretary added that the effect of s 6 was 'to create three categories, the first of which contains organisations which might be termed "obvious" public authorities, all of whose functions are public. The clearest categories are Government departments, local authorities and the police…The second category contains organisations with a mix of public and private functions…those organisations, unlike "obvious" public authorities, will not be liable in respect of their private acts. The third category is organisations with no public functions – accordingly they fall outside the scope of s 6.'

3.7.6   There are, however, a number of problems with this explanation. First, so far as providing any clarity about organisations beyond the 'obvious', the response is rather akin to saying, when asked to describe an elephant, 'Well, you'll recognise one if it stands on your toe.' Second, although the 'obvious' may well be obvious in some cases, it may be less so in others, especially if the functions being exercised are more in the nature of private functions, for example and in particular, in respect of contracts of employment [see *Evans v The University of Cambridge* [2002] EWHC 1382 (Admin), which is considered in paragraph 3.7.14 below]. Third, it did not mention the concept of 'horizontality', a device which may be used to extend Human Rights Act principles beyond the public sector in any event. And fourth it forgot the courts' ability, nay apparent desire, to impose duties on 'obvious' public authorities by creating indirect liabilities over the private acts of private bodies where a contractual relationship exists between a public authority and a private body [see *R v Leonard Cheshire Foundation* [2002] EWCA Civ 366 and 3.7.18 below].

3.7.7   Turning to the first category of public authorities – what might be termed the Basil or Sybil Fawlty categorisation of public bodies: of which organisations would it be 'bleeding obvious' to state that they perform functions of a public nature? The Home Secretary identified central Government departments, local authorities and the police and they are fairly obviously public authorities when exercising their functions with regard to members of the public. Local education authorities would likewise be caught, along with the governing bodies of maintained schools which derive their authority and functions from statute. Adjudicators and school organisation committees would also appear to be obvious and independent appeal panels, whether established by LEAs or governing bodies of foundation or voluntary aided schools, would fall within the definition (and, indeed, no argument has been made, in the human rights cases brought against their decisions, that they are not within the s 6-definition – see, for example, *S, T, P v Oxfordshire County Council and Others* [2002] EWCA Civ 693). There may be areas, such as employment, where, as we will see, the issues may not be clear cut, but in the main we can agree with the Home Secretary that these are obvious public bodies.

3.7.8   The less obvious ones, though, are where difficulties will arise and, in the educational context, will include independent and non-maintained schools,

3.7.9   The test is not: is this authority public? Except in the case of courts and tribunals, the test is whether 'any person, certain of whose functions are of a public nature' [s 6(3)(b) Human Rights Act] is a public authority *but* subject to the provision that 'in relation to a particular act, a person is not a public authority by virtue of being a person certain of whose functions are of a public nature if the nature of the act is private' [s 6(5) Human Rights Act]. This suggests that whatever category the organisation may, on its face, fall into, with the exception of courts and tribunals which are deemed always to be public authorities, there is room for argument that, because of the nature of the function during the exercise of which it is claimed Convention Rights are infringed, even an 'obvious' public authority may not be considered as a public authority for the purposes of the 1998 Act.

3.7.10 This is perhaps a not very obvious consequence of the wording of s 6 and may not have been intended, but taking an example may help explain the point. A local education authority employs an education welfare officer to enforce school attendance and issue proceedings for non-attendance under s 444 of the Education Act 1996. There is no doubt that, by the 'bleeding obvious' criteria, the function for which the EWO is employed is public in nature. If, however, during the course of her employment, the EWO is alleged to have made a racist comment, is dismissed by the LEA but subsequently claims that the LEA infringed her Convention Right to free expression (Article 10), is it open to the LEA to argue that it is not a public authority and therefore the Convention Rights cannot be invoked against it in the context of the contract of employment?

3.7.11 Initially, this argument would appear to have little merit. As the Fawltys would say, 'it's bleeding obvious' that the LEA is a public authority, therefore it must be under the duty to act compatibly with its employees' Convention Rights. Or is it? But, and this may be a big but, s 6(5) says that *in relation to a particular act* (here, the dismissal), a person (which includes a statutory corporation i.e. the LEA) is not a public authority *by virtue only of being a person certain of whose functions are functions of a public nature* (bleeding obviously the LEA has certain functions of a public nature) *if the nature of the act is private.*

3.7.12 Under pre-1998 Act case law, it was well established that certain contractual relationships, usually contracts of employment, with local authorities or similar bodies were private in nature and public law proceedings, principally judicial review, could not be used to enforce the contract or obtain remedies for breach [see, for example, *R v East Berkshire Health Authority ex p Walsh* [1985] QB 152, *McLaren v Home Office* [1990] IRLR 338 and *R v BBC ex p Lavelle* [1983] 1 WLR 23].

3.7.13 It would follow that if the function of employing staff, even if the power to employ is statutory (in the case of local authorities under s 112 of the Local Government Act 1972) has been held to be private, particular acts relating to employment relationships would fall within s 6(5) and therefore outside the s 6(1) duty. That idea appears to have been given short shrift, or perhaps not considered, in many of the texts but it has raised its head because of the decision of Scott Baker J in *Evans v The University of Cambridge* [[2002] EWHC 1382 (Admin)].

3.7.14 In *Evans*, a university lecturer sought judicial review of the University's refusal to offer her a promotion or create a personal professorship for her. Although the University was a creature of statute, deriving its powers from the Oxford and Cambridge Act 1923 and having power to make its own ordinances subject to the approval of the Privy Council, the court held that the public law process of judicial review was not appropriate to deal with a private law, employment dispute. '[T]he principle to be derived from the authorities and to be applied in a case such as the present is that the court has to look closely at the functions of the body whose decision is being questioned and if they are of a private or employment rather than a public nature there will ordinarily be no basis for the Administrative Court to entertain the dispute. The fact that the University has public functions and that its powers derive from statute will, in the circumstances, be neither here nor there.' The judge also drew an analogy with the reasoning of the Court of Appeal in the *Leonard Cheshire* case [see 3.7.18 below] to the effect that the background elements in that case of regulations and funding did not make the Leonard Cheshire Foundation a public authority.

3.7.15 Although *Evans* was not a human rights case, nonetheless, it may provide some support for the idea that whatever the nature of a body, whether established under statute or not, the question of whether or not it is a public authority will depend on the *particular* functions being exercised and that if the function is one of employment (or other analogous private law contractual right) it should be treated as private in nature and for that purpose therefore, the body, albeit 'public' will not be a 'public authority' for the purposes of the 1998 Act.

3.7.16 The argument may, however, be rendered somewhat academic either because the terms of the 1998 Act may be incorporated into the contracts of employment of public servants whether expressly or impliedly or because the concept of 'horizontality' [see paragraph 3.7.28 below] may mean that eventually human rights issues will be incorporated into the dealings of private bodies because of the way the courts and tribunals will be forced to comply with human rights principles, even in cases which do not involve public authorities. Nonetheless, given that the 1950 Convention was intended to prevent a state abusing the rights of its citizens, it might be fair to say that it should not be used to protect the employment rights of state employees, certainly where similar protections are not available to non-state employees or, indeed, office holders.

3.7.17 The applicability of the duty to hybrid organisations, such as, for example, city academies, independent schools and private sector providers of LEA services after interventions, was much discussed when the 1998 Act came into force. Whilst these organisations were *per se* private or private sector based, the question was asked whether the fact that they might perform certain functions or activities on behalf of a public authority, or were funded by a public authority to provide services, would bring them under the terms of the 1998 Act.

3.7.18 The point was considered and the definition of 'public authority' limited by the Court of Appeal in the case of *R v Leonard Cheshire Foundation* [[2002] EWCA Civ 366]. That case involved a charitable foundation which ran a nursing home for a number of older persons, most of whom had been placed at the home by local authorities under the National Assistance Act 1948. (Although this was therefore a social services case, nonetheless it is of general application as to the meaning of a 'public authority' but is anyway very similar to the situation of children placed in independent or non-maintained special schools under statements of SEN). The Foundation proposed to reorganise its homes which would have led to some of the residents being moved. They argued that they had been assured of a 'home for life' and that their forced removal would amount to an infringement of their Article 8 right to have their home and family life respected. To invoke Article 8, however, the residents first had to show that the Foundation was a public authority.

3.7.19 They failed. In the Court of Appeal's view, the role the Foundation was performing 'manifestly did not involve the performance of public functions. The fact that [the Foundation] is a large and flourishing organisation does not change the nature of its activities from private to public' [at paragraph 35]. The Court accepted that it was possible for an organisation like the Foundation to perform some public and some private functions. However, there was no distinction between the nature of the services provided to private residents at the home and publicly placed residents, other than the source of funding. 'While the degree of public funding of the activities of an otherwise private body is certainly relevant as to the nature of the functions performed, by itself it is not determinative of whether the functions are private or public.' There was no evidence of any other 'public flavour' to the activities of the Foundation as the Court held that it was not standing in the shoes of the local authorities, even though if a local authority had accommodated the residents in one of its own homes, the 1998 Act would have applied, nor was it exercising statutory powers in performing functions for the residents. A purely contractual relationship between a public body and a private organisation will therefore not be sufficient in itself to impose a s 6 duty on the private organisation.

3.7.20 This decision can be contrasted, however, with the decision of the Court of Appeal in *Poplar Housing and Regeneration Community Association Ltd v Donoghue* [[2001]LGR 489]. The organisation involved in this case was a housing association, a registered social landlord, created by a local authority and to which the local authority's housing stock had been transferred. The claimant was a tenant of a property in which he had originally been placed by the local authority's housing department, but whose tenancy was subsequently transferred to the housing association. Lord Woolf CJ, who also gave the leading judgment in *Leonard Cheshire*, had made clear that simply because a body performed a function which if it had not done so, a public body would have been under a duty to perform, did not render that private body susceptible to challenge under s 6.

3.7.21 'The purpose [at paragraph 59] of s 6(3)(b) is to deal with hybrid bodies which have both public and private functions. It is not to make a body, which does not have responsibilities to the public, a public body merely because it performs acts on behalf of a public body which would constitute public functions were such acts to be performed by the public body itself. An act can remain of a private nature even though it is performed because another body is under a public duty to ensure that that act is performed.'

3.7.22 This statement, and also his judgment in *Leonard Cheshire,* were based in part on the principle that a state or state authority cannot absolve itself from responsibility by delegating its obligations to private bodies or individuals. As Lord Woolf went on [at paragraph 60]:

> 'A useful illustration is provided by the decision of the European Court of Human Rights in *Costello-Roberts v United Kingdom* (1993) 19 EHRR 112. The case concerned a seven-year-old boy receiving corporal punishment from the headmaster of an independent school. The Court of Human Rights made it clear that the state cannot absolve itself of its Convention obligations by delegating the fulfilment of such obligations to private bodies or individuals, including the headmaster of an independent school. However, if a local authority, in order to fulfil its duties, sent a child to a private school, the fact that it did this would not mean that the private school was performing public functions. The school would not be a hybrid body. It would remain a private body. The local authority would, however, not escape its duties by delegating the performance to the private school. If there were a breach of the Convention, then the responsibility would be that of the local authority and not that of the school.'

As we will see, it therefore seems implicit from his judgment in *Leonard Cheshire* that there may be circumstances where a public authority is obliged to 'pass on', albeit not delegate, its obligations via a contract.

3.7.23 In contrast to the Foundation in *Leonard Cheshire*, the Court though held that the Poplar Housing Association was a public authority. The logic of the distinction is, however, readily apparent when the nature of a housing association is considered. As Lord Woolf continued [at paragraph 65]:

> 'In coming to our conclusion as to whether Poplar is a public authority within the Human Rights Act 1998 meaning of that term, we regard it of particular importance in this case that:
>
> (i)　While s 6 of the Human Rights Act 1998 requires a generous interpretation of who is a public authority, it is clearly inspired by the approach developed by the courts in identifying the bodies and activities subject to judicial review. The emphasis on public functions reflects the approach adopted in judicial review by the courts and textbooks since the decision of the Court of Appeal ... in *R v Panel on Take-overs and Mergers, ex p Datafin plc* [1987] QB 815.
>
> (ii)　Tower Hamlets, in transferring its housing stock to Poplar, does not transfer its primary public duties to Poplar. Poplar is no more than the means by which it seeks to perform those duties.

(iii) The act of providing accommodation to rent is not, without more, a public function for the purposes of s 6 of the Human Rights Act 1998. Furthermore, that is true irrespective of the section of society for whom the accommodation is provided.

(iv) The fact that a body is a charity or is conducted not for profit means that it is likely to be motivated in performing its activities by what it perceives to be the public interest. However, this does not point to the body being a public authority. In addition, even if such a body performs functions that would be considered to be of a public nature if performed by a public body, nevertheless such acts may remain of a private nature for the purpose of ss 6(3)(b) and 6(5).

(v) What can make an act, which would otherwise be private, public, is a feature or a combination of features which impose a public character or stamp on the act. Statutory authority for what is done can at least help to mark the act as being public; so can the extent of control over the function exercised by another body which is a public authority. The more closely the acts that could be of a private nature are enmeshed in the activities of a public body, the more likely they are to be public. However, the fact that the acts are supervised by a public regulatory body does not necessarily indicate that they are of a public nature. This is analogous to the position in judicial review, where a regulatory body may be deemed public but the activities of the body which is regulated may be categorised private.

(vi) The closeness of the relationship which exists between Tower Hamlets and Poplar. Poplar was created by Tower Hamlets to take a transfer of local authority housing stock; five of its board members are also members of Tower Hamlets; Poplar is subject to the guidance of Tower Hamlets as to the manner in which it acts towards the defendant.

(vii) The defendant, at the time of transfer, was a sitting tenant of Poplar and it was intended that she would be treated no better and no worse than if she remained a tenant of Tower Hamlets. While she remained a tenant, Poplar therefore stood in relation to her in very much the position previously occupied by Tower Hamlets.'

3.7.24 At paragraph 66, he continued

'While these are the most important factors in coming to our conclusion, it is desirable to step back and look at the situation as a whole. As is the position on applications for judicial review, there is no clear demarcation line which can be drawn between public and private bodies and functions. In a borderline case, such as this, the decision is very much one of fact and degree. Taking into account all the circumstances, we have come to the conclusion that while activities of housing associations need not involve the performance of public functions, in this case, in providing accommodation for the defendant and then seeking possession, the role of Poplar is so closely assimilated to that of Tower Hamlets that it was performing public and not private functions. Poplar therefore is a functional public authority, at least to that extent. We emphasise that this does not mean that all Poplar's functions are public. We do not even decide that the position would be the same if the defendant was a secure tenant. The activities of housing associations can be ambiguous. For example, their activities in raising private or public finance could be very different from those that are under consideration here. The raising of finance by Poplar could well be a private function.'

3.7.25 The conclusion from these two cases would appear to be that where a private organisation 'takes over' the responsibilities of a public authority following a transfer (whether statutory or otherwise) it will be regarded as a public authority, especially if links are still maintained with the transferor body. For example if a local authority has seats on the board of the organisation or the local authority can direct the organisation how to operate. This, again, appears to have logic. If one day, a function is carried out by a council, but next day is transferred to the private sector, why should service users suddenly find themselves deprived of the ability to enforce their Convention Rights? In the education context this may become important, especially with the new framework models for both schools ands LEAs and private sector intervention in LEAs, where those companies which take on an LEA's or school's statutory function may therefore be treated as 'public authorities' and probably should be. This belief is supported by the recent decision of Field J in *R v Hampshire Farmers Market Ltd ex parte Beer* [[2002] EWHC 2559 Admin]. In that case, a local authority had set up a company limited by guarantee to which it had transferred its functions of organising farmers' markets. The Court held that as the company had effectively 'stepped into the shoes' of the authority, it was a public authority for the purposes of s 6.

3.7.26 In contrast, where the relationship with the private organisation is contractual only, for example the placement of elderly persons or more relevantly, the placement of children in independent or non-maintained schools, the fact that they may be publicly funded does not provide them with the ability to enforce their Convention Rights vis-à-vis the private organisation.

3.7.27 The protection for these persons, however, and one of the reasons why the Court of Appeal in *Leonard Cheshire* felt able to find against the residents [see paragraph 33], is that the local authority cannot divest itself of its Convention obligations by contracting out to voluntary sector providers. It would, or so the Court of Appeal thought, be possible for a resident (or placed child) to require the local authority to enter into a contract with its provider which fully protected the resident's Convention Rights. Although there may be privity of contract issues, as the contract will be between the authority and provider and the resident will not therefore be a party, the Court nonetheless felt that this would provide sufficient protection as 'not only could the local authority rely on the contract, but possibly the resident could do so also as a person for whose benefit the contract was made'. The lesson for local authorities must therefore be that when contracting with outside providers, a term must be included within the contract requiring the provider to act in a manner which is compatible with the Convention Rights of the person to whom it is providing the service. If they do not, the local authority will have continuing obligations towards the individual for whom it is responsible and if the provider abuses that person's Convention Rights, the likely action under the 1998 Act will be against the local authority not the provider. That may be fine in principle but it will depend upon the opportunity being available to introduce such contractual terms and the willingness of outside providers to accept them. In areas where demand is high, such as residential accommodation for older persons and specialised residential placements, where potentially issues of human rights may be most relevant, providers may be reluctant to take on such obligations or the cost of securing insurance may be an additional burden which could reduce an already dwindling number of providers.

3.
FUNDAMENTAL
PRINCIPLES

3.7.28 The other factor which might, in any event, impose Human Rights Act duties on the private sector is the principle known as 'horizontality'. The 1998 Act is primarily (in some views, solely) concerned with applying direct duties onto public authorities, what is known as applying vertically. Horizontality, in contrast, is the argument that duties under the Human Rights Act may be applied as between individuals, who may not in themselves be public authorities. This argument is based upon the obligation imposed on courts and tribunals by s 3 of the 1998 Act to interpret legislation in a way which is compatible with Convention Rights and not to act in a way which is incompatible with Convention Rights [s 6 Human Rights Act]. It follows, so the argument goes, that if individuals who are not public authorities, appear before courts and tribunals (and this may be particularly relevant in the employment context), their claim must be determined by the courts or tribunals to ensure that their Convention Rights are not infringed. Thus, if a court were to determine a claim, say, for breach of contract between an independent school and a pupil, although the 1998 Act would not apply directly (or vertically) against the independent school, horizontally it would for if the claim related to a person's Convention Rights, the court could not simply ignore them but would have to act compatibly with them, even if the school did not. The logic of this argument is that all citizens have the same, equal status under the Human Rights Act and that, in a world of increasing outsourcing, there is no rational reason why the idea that on day one, a person will have Convention Rights because the body they are dealing with is a public one, but that if, on day two, that body's functions are transferred to a private company, those rights will simply disappear. There is another interesting point here as to whether a person's Human Rights Act rights are rights and liabilities which transfer either under the statutory provision authorising the transfer or under the Transfer of Undertakings Regulations. On the other hand, the argument does cause uncertainty and could lead to private bodies being uncertain whether the Human Rights Act applies to them or not. If, as the Government professed when introducing the Act, however, its aim was truly to bring human rights home, perhaps horizontality should be, or should eventually be, a fundamental part of its ambition. If so, the nature of the parties and particularly whether the alleged perpetrator of the breach is a public authority may be of academic interest only.

3.8   Who may bring proceedings?

3.8.1   Assuming for the time being that the alleged transgressor is a public authority, the Human Rights Act does not enable everyone or everything to take action for breach of their Convention Rights. A person who claims that a public authority has acted in a manner which is incompatible with their Convention Rights may bring proceedings against the authority in the appropriate court or tribunal or may rely on that Convention Right in any proceedings brought against him or her [s 7(1) Human Rights Act]. However, to be eligible to make such a claim, the person must be a victim or potential victim of the unlawful act [s 7(1) Human Rights Act].

3.8.2   'Victim' has a special meaning and a person can therefore only bring a claim if he or she would be a victim for the purposes of Article 34 of the Convention if proceedings were brought in the ECtHR in respect of that act [s 7(7) Human Rights Act]. Article 34 provides that an application can be brought to the ECtHR only by 'any person, non-Governmental organisation or group of individuals claiming to be the victim of a violation by one of the [Parties to the Convention or through the 1998

Act, a domestic public authority] of the rights set forth in the Convention or the protocols thereto'.

3.8.3 This is therefore a rather different test from the one previously applied by domestic courts in the case of applications for judicial review with which UK lawyers have become familiar. As will be seen, the definition of 'victim' is arguably more restrictive than the concept of 'locus standi' which has previously been applied in the United Kingdom. [To bring an action for judicial review a person has to have sufficient 'locus standi' or interest in the proceedings. This is designed to avoid vexatious or meddling litigants bringing applications against public bodies and requires the person bringing the claim to show that they are interested in the facts of the case and its outcome. English domestic law has however been expanded to permit, for example, campaigning groups or representatives of such groups to bring proceedings – see, for example, *R (on the application of Quintavalle on behalf of Comment on Reproductive Ethics) v Human Fertilisation and Embryology Authority* [[2002] EWHC 2785 (Admin)].]

3.8.4 The ECtHR has not permitted 'concerned citizens' to bring proceedings because they believe something their Government is doing may infringe the Convention. Abstract challenges, however well-intentioned, have not been allowed [see, for example, *Klass v Federal Republic of Germany* (1978) 2 EHRR 214]. There must, at the very least, be an effect or potential effect of the public authority's act on the individual making the claim. Accordingly, and to bring judicial review in line with the 1998 Act, s 7(3) and (4) provide that, notwithstanding the fact that to bring a judicial review a claimant need only show that they have a sufficient interest, if a claimant alleges breach of Convention Rights in a judicial review application, they must also show that that they are or would be a 'victim' of the unlawful act.

3.8.5 Nonetheless, the purposive interpretation of Convention Rights does mean that courts should not be unduly restrictive in determining who is a victim. Thus individuals need not show that their rights *have been* violated; the test is whether *they run the risk of being directly affected by the action about which they complain* [see *Marckx v Belgium* (1979) 2 EHRR 330 and *Norris v Ireland* (1988) 13 EHRR 186]. Although potential victims may therefore be covered [in *Norris,* the claimant was a homosexual who protested at the Irish criminal law prohibiting homosexual relations between consenting adult males. He had not been prosecuted himself, but because he would run the risk of being so prosecuted, he was held to be a victim], the 'victim' must previously have asserted his or her right against the public authority [*Guenoun v France* 66 DR 181 (1990)] and normally should have utilised all available means of domestic challenge [*Vijayanathan and Pusparajah v France* (1992) 15 EHRR 62]. Although this latter point was established by the ECtHR in the context of a claim against a state, presumably it will take effect under the 1998 Act, in the sense that the courts will expect a claimant to have exhausted internal or statutory appeal mechanisms, except in very special circumstances, before launching court proceedings.

3.8.6   A claimant may, in certain circumstance, be an indirect victim, for example a close relative, and especially a parent on behalf of their child (as in, for example, *Campbell and Cosans v United Kingdom*).

3.8.7   Although non-Governmental organisations are specifically identified as potential victims, this is not an open door to pressure groups to bring tests cases or bring campaigning actions in the courts. Such an organisation cannot claim to be a victim simply because it argues it represents the interests of its members, subscribers or supporters [see *Purcell v Ireland* 70 DR 262 (1991)]. However, it may bring a claim if a public authority is infringing the organisation's 'own' Convention Rights, for instance, preventing it from lawfully associating or expressing opinions [for example, *CCSU v United Kingdom* 50 DR 228 (1987)], and, and perhaps most importantly, it may support individual members who are complaining about breaches of their own Convention Rights. Campaigning cases are therefore possible, provided the organisation can find a willing 'victim' whose cause it can support. Limited companies or limited liability partnerships, as well as partnerships and unincorporated associations may also be victims, provided that they are not themselves within the definition of public authority. For, and this is a main area where the 1998 Act differs from old fashioned judicial review, public authorities themselves cannot be victims as they do not fall within the Article 34 definition [see *Rothenthurm Commune v Switzerland* 59 DR 251 (1988) and *Ayuntamiento v Spain* 68 DR 209 (1991)]. Consequently, local authorities, LEAs and governing bodies of maintained schools will not be able to claim that they have Convention Rights which have been infringed. In 2001 rural head teachers in Worcestershire were reported as threatening to bring action against the Government under s 7 of the 1998 Act because of the alleged low levels of funding. Whether such a claim would have succeeded is debatable, but certainly the claim could not have been made by the schools (as public authorities) and it is debatable if the head teachers as individuals would have been affected sufficiently to make them victims [see *'Hard-up rural heads plan legal bid'*, *TES*, 23 November 2001 and they were still obviously contemplating similar action when the next year's budget was set, see *'Heads plan human rights challenge to funding'*, *The Independent*, 4 February 2002].

3.9   Bringing a claim

3.9.1   As has been seen, in order to overcome the initial hurdles to making a claim, a person must be able to show that they are the victim of a public authority. Any such proceedings must be brought (where the victim is instigating the action – if they are relying on their Convention Rights in defence of an action brought by a public authority against them, clearly such limitations do not apply) against the public authority before the end of the period of one year beginning with the date on which the act complained of took place, or such longer period as the court of tribunal considers equitable having regard to all the circumstances [s 7(5) Human Rights Act]. However, this period is subject to any rule of court imposing a shorter period, so if, for example, the claim had to be made through judicial review, the claim would have to be made promptly or in any event within three months of the act or omission [s 31(6) Supreme Court Act 1981].

3.9.2   In principle, the 1998 Act is prospective not retrospective. A person may not, therefore, rely on Convention Rights under the 1998 Act in relation to an act taking place before the coming into force of the Act, i.e. 1 October 2000 [s 22(4) Human Rights Act]. A 24 year old former pupil, for example, could not therefore bring a claim now under the 1998 Act against her primary school teacher for infringement of her rights 16 years ago. The only exceptions are where a person may rely on Convention Rights (i.e. in their defence) in any proceedings brought by or at the instigation of a public authority whenever the act in question took place [s 22(4) Human Rights Act].

3.9.3   This was thought to be uncontentious. However, difficulties have arisen in a number of contexts, for example where proceedings were brought before the 1998 Act came into force, but were not heard until afterwards or appeals against judgments made before 1 October 2000 were heard after that date. In *Pearce v Governing Body of Mayfield School* [2001] EWCA Civ 1347], a teacher claimed for sex discrimination in respect of acts of pupils taking place between 1994 and 1996. She launched an employment tribunal claim in 1996, the full hearing of which was held early in 1999. She appealed against that decision to the Employment Appeal Tribunal which heard the case in early 2000. She appealed that decision to the Court of Appeal, which heard the appeal in 2001 and as part of which and for the first time she introduced the claim that her Convention Rights had been breached. The Court of Appeal held that the teacher could not rely on her Convention Rights in those circumstances. The acts challenged had occurred before the 1998 Act came into force, her claim had been commenced before then and the fact that an appeal was held after commencement did not permit the court to look back to early acts and decisions with the benefit of 1998 Act hindsight. If the public authority had been bringing the claim (or more likely a prosecution) in respect of pre-1 October 2000 events, the situation would clearly have been different and the individual could have invoked her Convention Rights retrospectively.

3.10 Methods of challenge

3.10.1 Convention Rights can be invoked in three ways in domestic courts and tribunals. First, an alleged breach can be used in defence of or to resist an action brought against an individual by a local authority. This applies whether the action is criminal or civil. Second, if an individual is bringing a claim against a public authority, breach of Convention Rights can be added as an additional ground of challenge whether the proceedings are in the courts or any of the numerous tribunals; for example, a judicial review may be brought alleging that the public authority has acted in breach of its statutory duties under UK law. Since 1 October 2000, it would also be possible for the claimant to add grounds to the effect that the public authority has also infringed his human rights. Similarly, a claim for bullying might also now include, in addition to the standard pleading that the school/ LEA had been negligent, a ground that the school had failed to protect a pupil's Convention Rights, especially the right to be protected from inhuman or degrading treatment. Third, a 'stand alone' human rights claim can be brought in which the claimant, usually by judicial review, simply asserts that his Convention Rights have been infringed.

3.11 Remedies

3.11.1 Courts and tribunals are given considerable flexibility in offering remedies for breach of Convention Rights. Where a court or tribunal finds that any act, or proposed act of a public authority is, or would be, unlawful, it may grant such relief or remedy, or make such order within its powers as it considers just and appropriate [s 8(1) Human Rights Act]. Effectively, s 8 simply enables courts and tribunals to use any of the remedies already available to them; no new remedies are introduced.

3.11.2 Damages may be awarded, but only in proceedings in which orders for damages and compensation could previously have been made. Thus damages for breaches of Convention Rights could be ordered by courts hearing personal injury claims, courts dealing with judicial reviews and tribunals, such as the Employment Tribunal, which could make orders for compensation. They cannot, however, be awarded where there is no domestic jurisdiction to award compensation, for example, in the

Special Educational Needs and Disability Tribunal or independent appeal panels.

3.11.3 If a court or tribunal has power to award damages or compensation, nonetheless, no such award may be made unless, taking account of all the circumstances of the case, including any other relief or remedy granted or order made in relation to the act in question, and also taking into account any consequences of any decision in respect of that act, the court or tribunal is satisfied that the award is necessary to afford just satisfaction to the person in whose favour it is made [s 8(3) Human Rights Act]. In determining whether to award damages or the amount of the award, the court or tribunal must take into account the principles applied by the ECtHR in relation to the award of compensation [s 8(4) Human Rights Act]. This qualification will, in effect, limit the amount of compensation likely to be awarded as the ECtHR, whilst not exactly parsimonious, has limited financial awards and if its decisions are to be followed, damages for breach of Convention Rights are likely to be far less in UK courts and tribunals than damages for other breaches of duty.

3. FUNDAMENTAL PRINCIPLES

3.11.4 As domestic remedies are to be used to provide relief, other sanctions will also be available. This will therefore include injunctions, quashing orders, mandatory orders, prohibiting orders and declarations, provided, of course, that the court or tribunal has the domestic jurisdiction to make such orders. In addition, as referred to above, the higher courts also have the power to make declarations of incompatibility [s 4 Human Rights Act] with the potential for remedial orders [s10].

3.12 Proportionality and judicial deference

3.12.1 A consideration of the general principles of human rights would not be complete without looking at the often mentioned principles of proportionality and margin of appreciation/judicial deference.

3.12.2 Proportionality, as will be seen, is a concept associated with the non-absolute Convention Rights and the principle that in certain cases the state or public authority's interference with a person's rights can be justified if necessary in a democratic society, is in accordance with the national law and properly balances the interest of the state with those of the individual. In effect, the courts will have to ensure that there is a fair balance between the interest or needs of society and the rights of the individual.

3.12.3 This is reflected in the notion that the acts of a state must be 'proportionate to the legitimate aim pursued' [see *Handyside v United Kingdom* (1976) 1 EHRR 737]. This has been interpreted to mean that a state or public authority will act proportionately only if its acts meet three criteria [see *Fayed v United Kingdom* (1994) 18 EHRR 393 and *De Frietas v Permanent Secretary of Ministry of Agriculture, Fisheries, Lands and Housing* [1998] 3 WLR 675, PC]:

a) the objective of the legislation, which provides the power to the state or public authority, must be sufficiently important to justify limiting a fundamental right;

b) the measures designed to meet the legislative objective must be rationally connected to the objective and cannot be arbitrary, unfair or based on irrational considerations; and

c) the means used to achieve those objectives and thus to interfere with the fundamental right must be no more than is necessary to accomplish the legitimate object.

3.12.4 Judicial deference is a related concept that derives from the ECtHR's adoption of the principle of allowing a 'margin of appreciation'. This principle was adopted from an early stage by the ECtHR as recognition that there were certain measures which should lie within a state's discretion and a European court should be loath to interfere in matters which were legitimately based on local customs, needs and conditions and where clearly the state had greater knowledge and understanding.

3.12.5 The 'margin of appreciation' principle cannot, however, be applied by domestic courts as, obviously, they should have the knowledge of national custom and Governmental discretion which the ECtHR lacks. Some commentators initially suggested that this meant the principle could never apply in the UK once the 1998 Act was brought into force.

3.12.6 However, the courts have adapted the principle to bring it more into line with the traditional reluctance of the courts in judicial review cases to interfere in matters of political discretion. As opposed to judicial review cases, where the court should be looking only at the procedures and powers adopted, not the merits of the decision challenged itself, the 1998 Act will require courts to look more closely at the body's decision and substitute its own opinion. The courts have therefore adopted the principle known as 'judicial deference' in the human rights context, where they believe that in certain circumstances they should defer to the legislature or the views of the public authority under scrutiny. The use of judicial deference and the circumstances in which courts should defer were first considered in detail after the 1998 Act had come into force by Laws LJ in *International Transport Roth GmbH v Secretary of State for the Home Department* [[2002] EWCA Civ 158]. Having considered the previous case law on the degree of deference which the judges will pay, or the scope of the discretionary area of judgment which they will cede, Laws LJ identified [at paragraphs 83 to 87] four principles:

83. [The] *first* principle which I think emerges from the authorities is that greater deference is to be paid to an Act of Parliament than to a decision of the executive or subordinate measure ... Where the decision-maker is not Parliament, but a minister or other public or Governmental authority exercising power conferred by Parliament, a degree of deference will be due on democratic grounds – the decision-maker is Parliament's delegate – within the principles accorded by the cases. But where the decision-maker is Parliament itself, speaking through main legislation, the tension of which I have spoken is at its most acute. In our intermediate constitution the legislature is not subordinate to a sovereign text, as are the legislatures in 'constitutional' systems. Parliament remains the sovereign legislator. It, and not a written constitution, bears the ultimate mantle of democracy in the State.

84. The *second* principle is that there is more scope for deference 'where the Convention itself requires a balance to be struck, much less so where the right is stated in terms which are unqualified' (*per* Lord Hope in *Kebilene* [*R v DPP ex parte Kebilene and Others* [2000] 2 AC 326]. In the present case we are principally concerned with Article 6, which does not on its face require any balance to be struck: it contains no analogue of paragraph 2 in Articles 9–11, dealing with political rights. It is thus a context which militates against deference. But even here, there is no sharp edge. The right to a fair trial under ECHR Article 6(1) is certainly unqualified and cannot be abrogated. So also is the presumption of innocence (in a criminal case) arising under Article 6(2). But what is required for fairness, what is required to satisfy the presumption of innocence, may vary according to context. In relation to Article 6(2), see in particular *Salabiaku* 13 EHRR 379, in which the European Court of Human Rights held (paragraph 28) that presumptions of fact or law against the defence should be confined 'within reasonable limits which take into account the importance of what is at stake and maintain the rights of the defence'. Hence I think it misleading to describe Article 6 rights as 'absolute', an adjective which tends to suggest that the nature of such rights is uniform, the same for every class of case (bar the distinction between civil and criminal). That is not right. The requirements of independence and impartiality are perhaps as close as one can get to uniform requirements. But even there, there may be scope for

reasonable differences of view as to the conditions which have to be met. What is the degree of security of tenure that a judge must enjoy if he is to constitute a tribunal compliant with Article 6(1)? At all events, however, Article 6 is an area where the deference due to the democratic powers is limited, since the rights it guarantees are unqualified.

85. The *third* principle is that greater deference will be due to the democratic powers where the subject-matter in hand is peculiarly within their constitutional responsibility, and less when it lies more particularly within the constitutional responsibility of the courts. The first duty of Government is the defence of the realm. It is well settled that executive decisions dealing directly with matters of defence, while not immune from judicial review (that would be repugnant to the rule of law), cannot sensibly be scrutinised by the courts on grounds relating to their factual merits...

86. Now this is not a case, of course, in which the courts are intruding in defence policy [the case was concerned with the fines imposed on hauliers who brought illegal immigrants into the UK], or the democratic powers in the rule of law. There are no tanks on the wrong lawns. But ... the constitutional responsibility of the democratic powers particularly includes the security of the State's borders, thus including immigration control, and that of the courts particularly includes the doing of criminal justice. If the scheme of the 1999 Act [Immigration and Asylum Act] is essentially to be treated as an administrative scheme for the betterment of immigration control in a context – clandestine entrants in vehicles – acknowledged to be especially acute, the courts will accord a much greater deference to Parliament in deciding whether there is any violation of Convention rights than if it is to be regarded as a criminal statute. In the latter case, the courts are of course obliged to apply Article 6(2) and (3) as well as (1). They would do so rigorously, with much less deference to the legislature, not only in fulfilment of their duty under the Human Rights Act but also because their own constitutional responsibility makes the task a necessarily congenial one...

87. The *fourth* and last principle is very closely allied to the third, and indeed may be regarded as little more than an emanation of it; but I think it makes for clarity if it is separately articulated. It is that greater or lesser deference will be due according to whether the subject-matter lies more readily within the actual or potential expertise of the democratic powers or the courts. Thus, quite aside from defence,

government decisions in the area of macro-economic policy will be relatively remote from judicial control: see, for example, *Ex p. Nottinghamshire CC* [1986] AC 240 and *Ex p. Hammersmith and Fulham LBC* [1991] 1 AC 521. Though these were not, of course, human rights cases, like problems as to the deference due to the democratic decision-maker arise in relation to the proper intensity of judicial review in other contexts, such as were there in play. In the present case, I have no doubt that the social consequences which flow from the entry into the United Kingdom of clandestine illegal immigrants in significant numbers are far-reaching and in some respects complex. While the evidence before us gives more than a flavour of the problems, the assessment of these matters (and therefore of the pressing nature of the need for effective controls) is in my judgment obviously far more within the competence of Government than the courts.'

3.12.7 These principles suggest that in the type of challenges with which schools or LEAs will be involved, deference will have little relevance. Courts will probably consider them outside the realm of areas such as national security or macro-economics. However, if the courts felt that, as they have said in a number of cases, especially those involving SEN [see, for example, *Bromley LBC v C and Special Educational Needs Tribunal* [[1999] ELR 260, CA], that educational decisions are best left to the educationalists, it is conceivable that judicial deference, whether expressed as such or not, may feature in future education human rights cases.

4. The Convention Rights

4.1 The Convention Rights generally

4.1.1 As has been seen, the Human Rights Act incorporates some, but not all, of the rights set out in the European Convention on Human Rights into UK law. Before considering how the functions of LEAs and schools have been affected or may be affected by that incorporation, it is briefly worth considering each individual Convention Right. Although many will not, on their face, appear to apply in the educational context, it is, nonetheless, worth knowing of their existence and effect not only for general information, but also because it is always possible that they may have an impact on LEAs or schools in ways not initially foreseen or envisaged. Because of its particular relevance, the Right to Education, contained in Article 2 of the First Protocol is considered separately in the next chapter.

4.1.2 The Convention Rights fall into three types of right: absolute rights, rights with defined limitations and qualified rights.

Absolute rights

4.1.3 Absolute rights, as the name suggests, are rights which cannot be qualified. They are the most fundamental of the fundamental rights and should not therefore be limited in any way nor should elements of proportionality or judicial deference enter the equation. Articles 2 (right to life), 3 (freedom from torture or inhuman and degrading treatment) and 4 (the freedom from forced and compulsory labour) fall into this category.

4.1.4 However, these rights do have specific exclusions built in. Thus, the guarantee of freedom from forced labour does not apply to prisoners, military service or normal civic obligations and a number of exclusions, such as self-defence, apply to Article 2.

4.1.5 Non-absolute rights (the limited and qualified rights combined) are still fundamental rights, but ones where, in certain circumstances, state interference or infringement may be justified in the interests of society.

Rights with defined limitations

4.1.6 These rights are the right to liberty (Article 4), the right to a fair trial (Article 6) and the right to marry and found a family (Article 12). With these, infringement of the right is permitted provided it falls within one or more of the defined circumstances where such an interference may be permissible. For example, in the case of the right to liberty, clearly that right should be, and is, limited so that an individual can lawfully be deprived of his or her liberty after conviction by a competent court.

Qualified rights

4.1.7   Qualified rights are expressed in two parts. First of all, an article will assert the right and the second part will acknowledge that there are permissible qualifications to the right. The article will then list the different considerations which may be taken into account in judging whether the qualification is justified.

4.1.8   Although all the qualifications differ slightly, a typical qualification is that the right may be infringed where it is 'necessary in a democratic society' in the interests of a variety of factors including national security, economic well-being, the protection of health or morals or, importantly when the victim's asserted rights need to be balanced with those of others, for the protection of the rights and freedoms of those other individuals.

4.2   Article 2 Right to life

1.   Everyone's right to life shall be protected by law. No one shall be deprived of his life intentionally save in the execution of a sentence of a court following his conviction of a crime for which this penalty is provided by law.

2.   Deprivation of life shall not be regarded as inflicted in contravention of this Article when it results from the use of force which is no more than absolutely necessary:

a)   in defence of any person from unlawful violence

b)   in order to effect a lawful arrest or to prevent the escape of a person lawfully detained

c)   in action lawfully taken for the purpose of quelling a riot or insurrection.

4.2.1   This, not surprisingly, is the most fundamental right in the whole Convention. It is absolute, although the three exclusions are permitted where absolutely necessary. Although similar to domestic law principles, such as self-defence, they are not exactly the same.

4.2.2   Obligations under this article are positive, as well as negative, in the sense that, as well as not killing its citizens, the state should also act to secure their adequate protection from non-state agents. Thus, a state is required to provide effective criminal laws to deter the commission of life-threatening offences.

4.2.3 Although used to challenge deaths in custody, the failure to prevent a murder and other such capital crimes, the Article has gained much publicity for its use in cases relating to medical treatment (or rather the discontinuance of treatment) [for an example of a pre-Human Rights Act case see *R v Collins; Pathfinder Mental Health Services NHS Trust and St Georges Healthcare NHS Trust ex parte S* [1998] EWHC Admin 490], euthanasia [*Pretty v United Kingdom* Application No 2346/02, 29 April 2002], abortion and, specifically the separation of Siamese twins [*A (Children)* [2000] EWCA Civ 254].

4.2.4 The Article means that health care must be provided, but the minimum level required has not been stated beyond requiring that the care must be sufficiently adequate to protect life [*Association X v United Kingdom* 4 DR 31 (1978)]. Before the introduction of the 1998 Act, UK courts had taken the view that the allocation of resources, even where there was a failure to allocate particular funding for the treatment of an individual whose life expectancy would be reduced without that treatment, was a matter for the proper authorities, not the courts – in effect an application of judicial deference [see 3.12.1*ff above*].

4.2.5 However, a failure to provide health care is very different from deliberately administering treatment knowing it will increase the probability of death. This has obviously arisen in the context of decisions on euthanasia, including decisions to turn off life support systems or cease to provide treatment, as well as more 'traditional' forms of assisted suicide.

4.2.6 Abortion is another contentious issue, but the ECtHR has preferred to leave the matter to the national courts to reflect attitudes in each country. The article does not however render abortion illegal, although it is not clear if the ECtHR's rationale is that unborn babies do not fall within the description of 'everyone' in the article or because it has introduced a *de facto* exclusion to the article, balancing the threat to the health of the mother against the rights of the foetus.

4.3 Article 3 Prohibition of torture and of inhuman or degrading treatment or punishment

No one shall be subjected to torture or to inhuman or degrading treatment or punishment.

4.3.1   This is another fundamental right, absolute and primarily designed to prevent the abuse of prisoners or the systematic use of torture. In fact, it is even more absolute than Article 2 as no derogation is permitted from its provisions, even in time of war. Although subject to no exclusions, the article requires the mistreatment to be above a particular threshold of severity.

4.3.2   This threshold of severity is, however, relative. It will therefore depend on the age, sex, vulnerability and state of health of the victim, the duration of the abuse and its consequences, both physical and mental. Thus, in the case of children the threshold is likely to be far lower than in the case of an adult male, although in *Costello-Roberts v United Kingdom* [(1993) 19 EHRR 112], the ECtHR held that the use of a slipper by a head teacher three times on a seven year boy was not sufficiently severe. However, a more violent application of, for example, a cane or treatment of a type being revealed by the all too prevalent enquiries into abuse at residential schools and homes, probably would have passed the threshold.

4.
CONVENTION
RIGHTS

4.3.3   The infliction of physical harm is not always necessary. Thus actions which lead to mental suffering will also fall within the article, so long as a sufficient degree of severity is reached [*Ireland v United Kingdom* (1978) 3 EHRR 25]. The threat of mistreatment may also amount to a breach of the article, provided it is real and immediate, although the threat of corporal punishment in a school did not pass the threshold [see *Campbell and Cosans v United Kingdom* (1982) 4 EHRR 293].

4.3.4   The various types of mistreatment identified in the article are, effectively, listed in order of severity. Thus the ECtHR has considered torture to mean deliberate inhuman treatment causing very serious and cruel suffering [*Ireland v United Kingdom* (1978) 3 EHRR 25]. Degrading treatment at the other end of the scale (though still sufficiently serious to meet the threshold) will arouse in the victim feelings of fear, anguish and inferiority capable of humiliating and debasing him or her and possibly breaking his physical or moral resistance [*Ireland v United Kingdom* (1978) 3 EHRR 25]. How this article may apply in the case of bullying is considered extensively in Chapters 8 and 13 below.

4.3.5   Punishment will be degrading if it entails a degree of humiliation and debasement which attains a particular level, and which is different from the usual element of humiliation which is usually involved in the punishment. Thus, although imprisonment for a crime can be humiliating, it won't be degrading where it is in accordance with normal, modern standards. Similar principles should apply in the case of school detentions.

4.4 Article 4 Prohibition of slavery and forced labour

1. *No one shall be held in slavery or servitude*

2. *No one shall be required to perform forced or compulsory labour*

3. *For the purpose of this Article the term 'forced or compulsory labour' shall not include:*

    (a) *any work required to be done in the ordinary course of detention imposed according to the provisions of Article 5 of this Convention or during conditional release from such detention;*

    (b) *any service of a military character or, in case of conscientious objectors in countries where they are recognised, service exacted instead of compulsory military service;*

    (c) *any service exacted in case of an emergency or calamity threatening the life or well-being of the community;*

    (d) *any work or service which forms part of normal civic obligations.*

4.4.1 This Article is a fundamental right and was aimed at preventing slavery, Gulag or Nazi work camps and sweat shop working conditions. The courts have therefore interpreted this article accordingly.

4.4.2 Slavery will cover the situation where a person is purportedly 'owned' by another and servitude involves a person being forced to work, but, in addition, is also forced to live on another's property where it is impossible for him or her to change their position [*Van Droogenbroeck v Belgium* (1980) Comm Report and (1982) 4 EHRR 443]. Forced and compulsory labour involves work exacted under the threat of a penalty of some sort and for which the individual has not volunteered.

4.4.3 And just to avoid any doubt, this does not normally apply to public sector workloads! The argument, presumably being that individuals work for local authorities and schools of their own free will, so the excess work is not forced upon them. In an ideal world, perhaps…

4.5 Article 5 Right to liberty and security of person

1. *Everyone has the right to liberty and security of person. No one shall be deprived of his liberty save in the following cases and in accordance with a procedure prescribed by law:*

    (a) *the lawful detention of a person after conviction by a competent court;*

   (b)   *the lawful arrest or detention of a person for non-compliance with the lawful order of a court or in order to secure the fulfilment of any obligation prescribed by law;*

   c)   *the lawful arrest or detention of a person effected for the purpose of bringing him before the competent legal authority on reasonable suspicion of having committed an offence or when it is reasonably considered necessary to prevent his committing an offence or fleeing after having done so;*

   d)   *the detention of a minor by lawful order for the purpose of educational supervision or his lawful detention for the purpose of bringing him before the competent legal authority;*

   (e)   *the lawful detention of persons for the prevention of the spreading of infectious diseases, of persons of unsound mind, alcoholics or drug addicts or vagrants;*

   (f)   *the lawful arrest or detention of a person to prevent his effecting an unauthorised entry into the country or of a person against whom action is being taken with a view to deportation or extradition.*

2.   *Everyone who is arrested shall be informed promptly, in a language which he understands, of the reasons for his arrest and of any charge against him.*

3.   *Everyone arrested or detained in accordance with the provisions of paragraph 1(c) of this Article shall be brought promptly before a judge or other officer authorised by law to exercise judicial power and shall be entitled to trial within a reasonable time or to release pending trial. Release may be conditioned by guarantees to appear for trial.*

4.   *Everyone who is deprived of his liberty by arrest or detention shall be entitled to take proceedings by which the lawfulness of his detention shall be decided speedily by a court and his release ordered if the detention is not lawful.*

5.   *Everyone who has been the victim of arrest or detention in contravention of the provisions of this Article shall have an enforceable right to compensation.*

4.5.1   This Article's aim is 'to ensure that no one should be dispossessed of [their physical] liberty in an arbitrary fashion' [*Engel v Netherlands* (1976) I EHRR 647]. There are however six fairly obvious grounds on which a state or public authority can deprive a person of this liberty. The most important being, equally obviously, the ability of the state to imprison a person properly convicted of an offence. So, the fact that under recent changes to the maximum sentence, a parent guilty of not securing their child's attendance at school can now be imprisoned, neither the prosecution nor the conviction should infringe this Article.

4.5.2 Typically the cases have involved the detention of prisoners and suspected criminals. A deprivation of liberty is required which goes beyond a mere restriction on movement. What will matter will be the type, duration, effects and manner of implementation of the restriction.

4.5.3 In the educational context, the issue which will leap immediately to mind is of lunch time or after school detention. Article 5 permits detention of a minor by lawful order for the purpose of educational supervision. This has been held to apply to an order remanding a child in custody provided educational facilities are provided at the earliest opportunity [*Bouamar v Belgium* (1987) 11 EHRR 1]. It should also apply to an order requiring a child to attend a particular school, i.e. an education supervision order, so that requiring that child to attend that school will not be a deprivation of his or her liberty.

4.5.4 That does not help though as far as a case of simple detention is concerned. 'Lawful order' could imply something more formal that a head teacher's decision to detain a child. On the other hand, provided the head teacher has complied with the conditions set out in s 550B of the EA 1996, he or she will be acting lawfully and he or she is issuing an order for the child to attend detention. Support for this latter argument can be found in *Nielsen v Denmark* [(1988) 11 EHRR 175], which permitted detention so long as the parent consented, even if the child objected. This seems a sensible way forward and one which will enable an appropriate disciplinary sanction, when properly carried out, to continue to be used. A note of caution though is that, as with many areas of education law, s 550B infers parental consent or that the lack of parental consent is immaterial provided the statutory conditions are met. It does not mention the consent of the child. In contrast, the UN Convention on the Rights of the Child provides for consultation with children on all decisions which affect them and offers protection against deprivation of liberty. School detention may, therefore, at some point be challenged, although if a school has met the s 550B conditions it is thought that such a challenge is unlikely to be successful.

4.6 Article 6 Right to a fair trial

1. In the determination of his civil rights and obligations or of any criminal charge against him, everyone is entitled to a fair and public hearing within a reasonable time by an independent and impartial tribunal established by law. Judgment shall be pronounced publicly but the press and public may be excluded from all or part of the trial in the interest of morals, public order or national security in a democratic society, where the interests of juveniles or the protection of the private life of the parties so require, or to the extent strictly necessary in the opinion of the court in special circumstances where publicity would prejudice the interests of justice.

2. *Everyone charged with a criminal offence shall be presumed innocent until proved guilty according to law.*

3. *Everyone charged with a criminal offence has the following minimum rights:*

   (a) *to be informed promptly, in a language which he understands and in nature and cause of the accusation against him;*

   (b) *to have adequate time and facilities for the preparation of his defence;*

   (c) *to defend himself in person or through legal assistance of his own choosing or, if he has not sufficient means to pay for legal assistance, to be given it free when the interests of justice so require;*

   (d) *to examine or have examined witnesses against him and to obtain the attendance and examination of witnesses on his behalf under the same conditions as witnesses against him;*

   (e) *to have the free assistance of an interpreter if he cannot understand or speak the language used in court.*

4.
CONVENTION
RIGHTS

4.6.1 Article 6 sets out an absolute right with certain limitations in terms of express qualifications, but also, in practice, as a result of interpretation of the words used. In effect the Article is little different from the domestic concept of natural justice, although, given the disputes to which the Article applies, the Article may actually be more limited in effect than UK law currently provides. As a fundamental right it was designed to avoid, on the one hand, the show trials of the Stalin era and, on the other hand, secret trials out of public gaze, meted out by state agents rather than independent tribunals.

4.6.2 The most important principle is that a person is entitled to a fair trial in proceedings which determine a criminal trial. This is of little relevance in the educational context, except in respect of prosecutions for non-attendance, breach of a school attendance order and employment bye-laws [see Chapters 7 and 8 below].

4.6.3 In the civil sphere, the Article provides the right to a fair trial in the determination of a person's civil rights and obligations. Before its subsequent provisions bite, therefore, there must be 1) a determination and 2) of civil rights and obligations.

4.6.4   A determination must comprise a result which is decisive of a person's rights and obligations. Preliminary opinions, decisions which need subsequent confirmation or ratification are therefore not determinations. And it must be a determination of civil rights and obligations. In this area, the ECtHR has adopted the European meaning of civil rights which can lead to somewhat surprising results. In particular, the ECtHR has not regarded as the 'right to a school place' such as it is, to be a civil right, with the consequence that a decision to refuse admission to a parent's preferred school is not a decision relating to a civil right, whether initially by the admissions authority or on appeal to an independent appeal panel [see, for example, *Simpson v United Kingdom* supra and *R v School Admissions Appeal Panel for Hounslow LBC ex parte Hounslow LBC* [2002] EWCA Civ 900 considered in chapters 6 and 8 below]. In fact, generally, the ECtHR has taken the view that public duties do not, by and large, give rise to civil rights protected by Article 6. Similarly, a dispute over public servants' recruitment, employment and retirement has generally been held to be outside the scope of the article as the ECtHR have considered it not to be a private civil right. This view is, however, diametrically opposed to the UK court's treatment of the contracts of public sector employees [and see Chapter 3 above], which are regarded as private law matters. It is possible therefore that if the issue is raised in the UK courts or tribunals they may depart from ECtHR precedent.

4.6.5   If Article 6 is invoked, then the protections listed come into play. Given the nature and number of UK tribunals and quasi-judicial panels, the requirement that the hearing must be an independent and impartial tribunal has exercised many lawyers and led to extensive litigation.

4.6.6   As is clear, we are not here talking solely about 'judicial' tribunals or bodies staffed solely by lawyers. All decision makers whether staffed by lawyers, civil servants, public officials, elected councillors or lay people will be covered provided that they have a judicial function, in that they have the power to consider all questions of fact and law; to determine matters within their jurisdiction and competence; and to make legally binding decisions; and are established by law, i.e. it should be established and regulated by Parliament rather than by the Government or a public authority.

4.6.7   That said, however, as long as it established by law, it is permissible for the Government to appoint members of these courts or tribunals. A fundamental principle is that these bodies should be independent and impartial, but that does not require an independent commission to make appointments to them. Thus, for example, it is considered permissible for the Secretary of State to appoint lay members of the Special

Educational Needs and Disability Tribunal and for the chairmen to be appointed by another minister, the Lord Chancellor. Care must be taken, however, to ensure that such appointees' terms of office and protections from removal do not undermine any theoretical independence. This was the problem faced by the Scottish court system when the use of Deputy Sheriffs appointed on an annual basis by the executive was held unlawful. As a result, the terms of appointment of part-time judges and tribunal chairmen have been changed to ensure that such bodies are Convention compliant.

4.6.8   A particular problem with part-time chairmen is that they may, often will, practise in the area of law with which the tribunal deals. This is not in itself a breach of the requirement of independence and impartiality [*Lawal v Northern Spirit Ltd* [2002] EWCA Civ 327] although obviously care must be taken. Fortunately, in the education context most panels and tribunals are already established to ensure that they are free of bias either by legislative requirement (in the case of independent appeal panels) or by adopted practice (in the case of the Special Educational Needs and Disability Tribunal). Nonetheless, if the issues arises, the test for impartiality is now laid down in the decision of the House of Lords in *Magill v Porter and Magill v Weeks* [[2002] 2 WLR 37]: 'The question is whether the fair-minded and informed observer, having considered the facts, would have concluded that there was a real possibility that the tribunal was biased' [per Lord Hope [2002] 2 WLR 37 at p84 and followed by the majority of the Court of Appeal in *Lawal*]. The aim must be to ensure that confidence of the parties and the public in the independence and impartiality of the courts is maintained [see, for example, *Sramek v Austria* (1984) 8 EHRR 351, *Veililos v Switzerland* (1988) 10 EHRR 466 and *Sengupta v The General Medical* Council [2002] EWCA Civ 1104].

4.6.9   Another potential obstacle to the independence of quasi-judicial tribunals is the fact that often they are required to have regard to Government guidance; for example, in the case of the SENDIST, the Tribunal must have regard to the Code of Practice on SEN, a code produced by the Secretary of State who appoints the two lay members of the Tribunal. Similarly, independent appeal panels must have regard to the relevant Codes of Practice and departmental guidance issued by the Secretary of State [though see *S, T, P v Oxfordshire County Council and Others* [2002] EWCA Civ 693]   for a consideration of the requirements imposed on panels by such guidance]. This problem was addressed, at least in part, in the *Alconbury* case [*R v Secretary of State for the Environment, Transport and the Regions, ex parte Alconbury Developments Ltd* [2001] UKHL 23; [2001] 2 WLR 1389]. That case related to the decision of a planning inspector, appointed by the

Secretary of State who had to have regard to, amongst other things, guidance issued by 'his' Secretary of State and who then reported to the Secretary of State, for the Secretary of State to take the decision. The House of Lords held that this system was not incompatible with Article 6 on the basis that a) even if the Secretary of State was not sufficiently independent and impartial, the fact that his decision was subject to control by courts that had full jurisdiction, provided adequate protection to ensure that the Article 6 rights were effective and b) it was entirely appropriate that the determination of a planning application in light of planning policy and guidance should be entrusted to members of the executive, such as the Secretary of State and/through his inspector, provided the Secretary of State was answerable to Parliament for policy issues and to the courts on legal issues. This case therefore appeared to quash the notion, which had been prevalent, that the availability of judicial review could not in itself make a tribunal or panel independent and impartial, as the court's jurisdiction in such proceedings is limited to consideration of the legal and procedural aspects of the case, not the merits.

4.6.10 This is of great importance in local Government. Many 'decisions' are made by quasi-judicial panels or, on occasion, individual officers acting under delegated powers. Judicial review is usually available to enable these decisions to be challenged. If, however, and assuming that these decisions constitute determinations of a person's civil rights, which is not always the case, judicial review can 'cure' any Article 6 defects in the original 'decision', local authorities will be able to carry on much as they have done before. If judicial review was not available, alternate mechanisms would be required to secure the necessary degree of independence and impartiality, either in the initial decision making or by providing an additional right of appeal. That in itself might not have cured these problems as, first, these 'tribunals' would have to be appointed by the authority, thus immediately questioning their independence, and, second, Article 6 requires tribunals to be established by law. As any new 'tribunals' created in response to this point would have been by nature extra-statutory, it would be hard to see how even these arrangements could meet the Article 6 deficit. Thankfully therefore, and although other judgments have been less keen on allowing judicial review or statutory appeals to be curative of potential Article 6 infringements, the House of Lords decision in *Alconbury* has at least introduced realism and avoided the need for local authorities to set up endless appeal processes with ever more panels.

4.6.11 The effect of this Article on particular education panels and tribunals is considered in more detail and in light of the specific case law in chapters 6 and 8 below.

4.7 Article 7 Freedom from retroactive criminal legislation

1. No one shall be held guilty of any criminal offence on account of any act or omission which did not constitute a criminal offence under national or international law at the time when it was committed. Nor shall a heavier penalty be imposed than the one that was applicable at the time the criminal offence was committed.

2. This Article shall not prejudice the trial and punishment of any person for any act or omission which, at the time when it was committed, was criminal according to the general principles of law recognised by civilised nations.

4.7.1 This Article contains two prohibitions: first, the prohibition of a retroactive application of criminal offences to punish conduct which was not criminal at the time the offences were committed. Second, it prohibits the retroactive increase in a penalty. This will be of little relevance in the education context and was introduced, principally, to prevent a new Government seeking 'revenge' on previous regimes. It does not, however, prevent the retrospective introduction of criminal legalisation addressing offences against the general principle of law recognised by civilised nations. In effect, then, the introduction of legislation relating to, for example, genocide and war crimes would not be unlawful under this Article.

4.8 Article 8 Right to respect for private and family life, home and correspondence

1. Everyone has the right to respect for his private and family life, his home and his correspondence.

2. There shall be no interference by a public authority with the exercise of this right except such as is in accordance with the law and is necessary in a democratic society in the interests of national security, public safety or the economic well-being of the country, for the prevention of disorder or crime, for the protection of health or morals, or for the protection of the rights and freedoms of others.

4.8.1 With most of the Convention Rights, UK law, to a greater or lesser extent, was compliant even before the 1998 Act was introduced. The predicted seismic shift in our law was never therefore as likely as some commentators suggested. However, as UK law did not recognise a right of privacy, Article 8 always had the potential to become the most innovative and effective right, and this has in practice proved to be the case. It is not just about privacy, but a number of high profile cases involving alleged celebrities have been brought and the media have, perhaps not unnaturally as the subject is so close to home, focused on the conflict between an individual's right to privacy and the press's so-called duty to publish what is in the public interest, including matters so vitally important to the welfare of the state as details of an unknown footballer's adventures with a lap dancer [*A v B and another sub nom Flitcroft v Mirror Group Newspapers Ltd* [2002] EWCA Civ 337], a newsreader's choice of swimwear [*Ford v The Press Complaints Commission* [[2001] EWHC Admin 683] and a model's trip to Narcotics, once but obviously no longer, Anonymous [*Campbell v Mirror Group Newspapers* [2002] EWCA Civ 1373], although so far the power of the press appears to have prevailed.

4.8.2   However, Article 8 is more than a right to privacy; indeed, it protects more than just private life, extending as it does to business communications so that its ambit is very wide, stretching over such complex legal and ethical problems as the right of sperm donors to be treated as parents [see, for example, *Rose and EM v Secretary of State for Health and the Human Fertilisation and Embryology Authority* [2002] EWHC 1593 (Admin) where the wish of a person born as a result of artificial insemination by anonymous donor to know details of their origin did engage Article 8] to the right of employers to bug their employees' phones and check their e-mail. Given the problems schools and LEAs have with parents, families and their rights and responsibilities, it is no wonder that this Article may be the most important in the education field and far outweigh the right to education in long term significance.

4.8.3   It should be noted from the start, however, that Article 8 does not impose a *right to privacy*. What, instead it does do is impose a right for a person to have their private and family life, their home and their correspondence *respected* by public authorities. And even that is subject to the qualification in Article 8(2) where interference is necessary in a democratic society.

4.8.4   As with many, if not most, articles, duties imposed on states and public authorities are both negative – i.e. a public authority must not act in a way which infringes the right – but also positive – in the sense that it should take steps to prevent others infringing the right. The positive is far easier for the state, as it could impose prohibitions on the media publishing certain information, than on public authorities, although these should take such measures as are within their power to prevent breaches, especially by their staff.

4.8.5   In broadening the concept of private life beyond mere privacy, i.e. the right not to be disturbed, Article 8 in effect provides individuals with the right to be themselves. Thus a person's wish to be gay should be respected under Article 8 [see, for example, *Dudgeon v United Kingdom* (1981) 4 EHRR 149], just as much as it should protect them from public authorities opening their correspondence or tapping their phones [see, for example, *Halford v United Kingdom* (1997) 24 EHRR 523]. The Article embraces respect for a person's physical and moral integrity, hence why cases challenging corporal punishment at school [*Costello-Roberts v United Kingdom* (1995) 19 EHRR 112] and at home [*A v United Kingdom* (1998) 5 BHRC 137] have been brought under it. It also embraces activities by public authorities, other than those directly interfering with an individual. Thus, planning development may infringe this right, as too may damage caused by pollution, including, potentially, noise pollution [*Rayner v United Kingdom* 47 DR 5 (1986)].

4. CONVENTION RIGHTS

4.8.6   Private life also includes the right to a personal identity. Individuals should therefore be entitled to gain access to records kept about them by public authorities, subject to the safeguards provided by the Article 8(2) qualifications. Thus, a man who had spent his childhood in local authority care was entitled to access to his records to see if he had been ill-treated whilst in care [*Gaskin v United Kingdom* (1989) 12 EHRR 36]. Respect for private and family life required that everyone should be able to establish details of their identity as individuals, including the right to obtain information about a biological parent [*Rose and EM v Secretary of State for Health and Human Fertilisation and Embryology Authority* [2002] EWHC 1593 (Admin)]. Sex, sexuality, sexual orientation and relationships are also part of a person's identity and therefore *prima facie* protected as well.

4.8.7   Private and family life is stated as being separate from the home. Hence, invasion of privacy away from the home is an infringement of the right, although taking photographs of individuals whilst in a public place is probably not an infringement [see *Friedl v Austria* (1995) 21 EHRR 83 and *Ford v Mirror Group Newspapers Ltd*].

4.8.8   Family life itself has, depending upon the timing and composition of the ECtHR, been given at time wide, at times more restricted meaning. It obviously relates to the relationship between husband and wife and parent and child and adoptive parents and adoptive child. It would also appear to apply to grandparents and uncles and aunts, although the particular circumstances of the relationship will be determinative of the question. More difficult are the different types of 'modern' relationship. Thus co-habiting partners of the opposite sex will be considered as family but although on occasion the ECtHR has taken a purposive approach, it has, nevertheless, not been willing to extend the ambit of 'family life' to a homosexual relationship (although the exclusion may be academic as such a relationship will nonetheless fall within the meaning of 'private life'). Similarly, a man who donated his sperm so that a lesbian could have a child by artificial insemination did not have a 'family life' with the baby [*G v Netherlands* (1993) 16 EHRR CD 38]. However, in *X, Y and Z v United Kingdom* [(1997) 24 EHRR 143], the ECtHR held that family life existed between a woman, her female to male transsexual partner and the child the woman had conceived by artificial insemination by an anonymous donor. The fact that the ECtHR had previously held [in *Kerkhoven v Netherlands* 19 May 1992] that family life did not exist between a non-biological parent and a child born as a result of artificial insemination to a lesbian and her lesbian partner shows that this Convention Right, perhaps more than any other, is subject to re-interpretation in light of society's changing attitude towards relationships.

4.
CONVENTION
RIGHTS

4.8.9   The ECtHR has been particularly protective of family life where the state has sought to take children away from their parents. However, the Article is not a veto on child care proceedings; public authorities must, however, be able to demonstrate justification for their draconian action and especially ensure that they can show the child's interests in being removed, outweigh those of their parent or the family [see *W v United Kingdom* (1987) 10 EHRR 29].

4.8.10   As with 'private life' the concept of 'home' has a wider meaning than normal. It therefore includes, as would be expected, a person's main residence [*Murray v United Kingdom* (1994) 19 EHRR 193] and a property purchased for future use. However, it also extends to a person's office or business premises [*Niemietz v Germany* (1992) 16 EHRR 97] as well as holiday caravans, hostel accommodation and unlawful occupation of land by gypsy caravans [*Buckley v United Kingdom* (1996) 23 EHRR 101].

4.8.11   Correspondence includes both written and verbal communication, thus telephone tapping is *prima facie* an interference [see *Halford v United Kingdom* (1997) 24 EHRR 523]. The gathering of information, whether on a computer database or in a manual filing system, also falls within this part of the Article, whether it comprises copies of, for example, letters, medical records, census information, details on the electoral roll or fingerprints. As a qualified right, of course, certain interference can be justified if it is in accordance with the law, for a legitimate aim and necessary in a democratic society for one or more of the reasons set out in Article 8(2).

4.8.12   A further aspect of the right to respect for private and family life accepted by the ECtHR is a person's right to establish and develop relationships with other human beings. Although, probably of little relevance in the education field, this was raised, though promptly dismissed by Newman J at first instance, in *R v Head Teacher of Alperton Community School and Others ex parte B and Others* [[2001] ELR at 389-390, QBD]. The argument put by the pupils' counsel was that placement in a pupil referral unit, as opposed to re-instating them into their 'old' school, could stop the development of their personality. Quite properly, it is suggested, this argument did not find favour.

4.9   Article 9 Freedom of thought, conscience and religion

1. *Everyone has the right to freedom of thought, conscience and religion; this right includes freedom to change his religion or belief and freedom, either alone or in community with others and in public or private, to manifest his religion or belief, in worship, teaching, practice and observance.*

2. *Freedom to manifest one's religion or beliefs shall be subject only to such limitations as are prescribed by law and are necessary in a democratic society in the interests of public safety, for the protection of public order, health or morals, or for the protection of the rights and freedoms of others.*

4.9.1   This qualified right provides protection against state persecution of religious minorities but also requires states to respect the religious and philosophical beliefs of its citizens, subject to the controls necessary in a democratic society. It also prevents the state imposition of particular beliefs.

4.9.2   The meanings of 'religion' and 'belief' have been widely interpreted, especially when including non-religious beliefs, for example, pacifism [*Arrowsmith v United Kingdom* 19 DR 5(1980)], on the basis that it is a philosophy. Humanism and atheism may, therefore, also enjoy certain protection.

4.9.3   In cases under this Article, the normal rules on 'victims' are modified, so that neither companies nor other incorporated or unincorporated associations can enjoy the right [*Church of X v United Kingdom* 12 YB 306 (1969)], as it should relate to personal beliefs. However, other decisions have held that a church may wish to protect its own beliefs and should be able to do so [*Chappell v United Kingdom* 53 DR 214 (1987)] and an organisation which is in reality no more than a collection of adherents can also enjoy the Article's protection. Thus a church should be able to enjoy these rights, whereas other organisations will not.

4.9.4   One of the most important decisions on this article was the Greek case of *Kokkinakis v Greece* [(1993) 17 EHRR 397]. The claimants were Jehovah's Witnesses who had been found guilty by the Greek courts of 'proselytism' after they sought to persuade others to join their sect. The ECtHR found that the right to manifest one's religion included trying to persuade others of the merits of a person's own religion or faith. 'Improper proselytism', however, i.e. something which goes beyond attempts at persuasion, would not be protected by Article 9.

4.9.5   Although the Article is qualified, only certain parts of the fundamental right can be limited by the state. The right to *hold* beliefs is wholly outside state interference; interference is permitted only to the *manifestation* of religion and belief. Thus the Article prohibits a state imposed requirement to hold particular views or thoughts or to disclose one's beliefs. No punishment can be imposed simply because a person believes in a particular religion or belief, provided it is not manifested in some form to another person or persons.

4.10   Article 10 Freedom of expression

1.   Everyone has the right to freedom of expression. This right shall include freedom to hold opinions and to receive and impart information and ideas without interference by public authority and regardless of frontiers. This Article shall not prevent States from requiring the licensing of broadcasting, television or cinema enterprises.

2.   The exercise of these freedoms, since it carries with it duties and responsibilities, may be subject to such formalities, conditions, restrictions or penalties as are prescribed by law and are necessary in a democratic society, in the interests of national security, territorial integrity or public safety, for the prevention of disorder or crime, for the protection of health or morals, for the protection of the reputation or rights of others, for preventing the disclosure of information received in confidence, or for maintaining the authority and impartiality of the judiciary.

4.10.1   This Article, which is associated with Articles 9 and 11, sets out the protections available to secure free expression or, at least, the free expression permissible in a democratic society and subject to the responsibilities society requires.

4.10.2   In contrast to Article 9, this freedom does not just apply to individuals or limited groups, such as churches. It can apply to all non-public authority entities as well, so, for example, it will apply to commercial organisations and the professions [see, for example, *Casado Coca v Spain* (1994) 18 EHRR 1 and *Jacubowski v Germany* (1994) 19 EHRR 244]. Expression embodies a wide variety of forms and is not just limited to the written or spoken word. Artistic works [*Muller v*

Switzerland (1988) 13 EHRR 212], images [*Chorherr v Austria* (1993) 17 EHRR 358] and, perhaps most importantly in the educational context, dress [*Stevens v United Kingdom* 46 DR 245 (1986)], have all been held to amount to expression. More disingenuous attempts to extend the meaning of expression have, however, been rejected. So preventing a prisoner from having sexual relations did not fall foul of Article 10, as the physical expression of feelings was held not to be within the Article [*Case of X* 19 DR 66 (1977)]. Whether this therefore excludes mime from a legitimate form of expression may be a moot point, although it may become less so if the issue concerns gestures provoked by annoyance. Is a child giving a 'V' sign to his or her teacher a case of an individual's free expression within the Article or just a case of bad behaviour?

4.10.3 State interference will, however, be justified under the qualifications where the expression exceeds what is permissible in a democratic society. This does not mean that simply because an expression offends, its prohibition may be justified, but does permit public authorities to take action against, for example, racist views or those advocating terrorism. The borderline between offensive expression which should be permitted and that which can be outlawed has, by and large, been left to the national courts, as standards may well vary between states. However, the ECtHR has been more protective of the right to express political views and has shown a lesser keenness to interfere in artistic or literary expression, which it feels should more appropriately be left to the domestic courts. The reticence of the Strasbourg court to comment upon the merits of a preserved cow, a pile of bricks or an unmade bed can perhaps be understood.

4.10.4 Impermissible interference with the freedom can be both pre- and post-expression, i.e. disciplinary action taken after an employee has said something his or her employer felt he or she should not say is just as unlawful as the prohibition against such statements in his or her contract of employment. The ECtHR has, however, stressed that prior, especially blanket, restraints require greater justification than actions taken in response to particular words or conduct.

4.10.5 Unusually, this Article does stress that although individuals have freedoms to express themselves, they also have duties and responsibilities. Courts and tribunals may, therefore, more so than with the other Articles, be required to balance the individual's freedom with the interests of other citizens and especially take account of the potential for the views expressed to offend. As indicated above, political opinions should be protected more actively, but the degree of offence caused by artistic and other expression can be judged by domestic courts and may, therefore, vary from state to state. The case law is therefore of little use and what may be found to be permissible in one state (for example the right of an artist to display paintings depicting sexual acts between men and animals in one country does not mean that all states must necessarily permit such expression [see *Muller v Switzerland* (1988) 13 EHRR 212 Muller v Switzerland (1988) 13 EHRR 212]). For example, in *Handyside v United Kingdom* [(1976) 1 EHRR 737], a publisher who had produced a book for children aged 12 upwards and which contained sex guidance and, in places, encouragement to experiment with drugs and sex was prosecuted for obscenity and the book banned. Although the book was a translation of a publication freely available elsewhere in Europe, the ECtHR did not find against the UK. Whilst stressing that in principle Article 10 was designed to protect publications, including those which would offend, shock or disturb a section of the population, the UK's actions on the facts were a proportionate and justifiable interference with the Article 10 freedom, were within the state's margin of appreciation and were necessary for the protection of the UK public's morals.

4.11 Article 11 Right to freedom of peaceful assembly and association

1. *Everyone has the right to freedom of peaceful assembly and to freedom of association with others, including the right to form and to join trade unions for the protection of his interests.*

2. *No restrictions shall be placed on the exercise of these rights other than such as are prescribed by law and are necessary in a democratic society in the interests of national security or public safety, for the prevention of disorder or crime, for the protection of health or morals or for the protection of the rights and freedoms of others. This Article shall not prevent the imposition of lawful restrictions on the exercise of these rights by members of the armed forces, of the police or of the administration of the State.*

4.11.1 This Article contains, in effect, two separate but related rights: the freedom to assemble for peaceful purposes and the freedom to associate with others. Association includes the freedom to form and join a trade union.

4.11.2 Freedom of assembly extends to meetings, gatherings, processions and marches in private and in public. Requiring prior approval before a march can take place is not in itself an infringement of the freedom, but clearly if approval was refused for impermissible reasons or conditions were imposed which rendered the freedom ineffective it is likely that a court would find the approving body in breach. The assembly must be 'peaceful' so, obviously, demonstrations with violent intent or which turn to violence are outside the protection of the Article. Again, the freedom, like the freedom of religion and beliefs and freedom of expression, places both passive and active duties on states and public authorities. Hence, not only can a state not interfere with the right without justification, but the state must also ensure that reasonable and lawful assemblies may take place without disruption.

4.11.3 Freedom of association primarily protects individuals who wish to join political parties or trade unions. Association implies 'a voluntary grouping for a common goal' [*Young, James and Webster v United Kingdom* (1982) 4 EHRR 38]. It does not, however, mean that an association is under an obligation to admit a person as a member, nor does it mean that an individual *must* associate. Consequently, an individual has the right not to join an association and the right not to be penalised for refusing. Thus dismissal of an employee because they refused to join a closed shop is an interference with this freedom [*Young, James and Webster v United Kingdom* [(1981) 4 EHRR 38]. However, requirements that a person must be a member of a particular professional body are not infringements of this freedom as the ECtHR has held that such bodies are not 'associations' for the purposes of Article 11 [*Le Compte, Van Leuven and De Meyere v Belgium* A 43 (1981) 4 EHRR 1, although why professionals can be required to join a closed shop whilst others cannot is a moot point, perhaps best answered by the fact that judges of the ECtHR are not noted for being members of trade unions but may have greater familiarity with organisations such as the Bar Councils and or the Law Society].

4.11.4 Interestingly, in view of the discussion as to whether public authorities are subject to the 1998 Act when acting as employers [see Chapter 3 above], the ECtHR has held that a state or public body acting as an employer is subject to control under Article 11 [*Swedish Engine Drivers' Union v Sweden* (1976) 1 EHRR 617 and *Schmidt Dahlstrom v Sweden* (1976) 1 EHRR 632]. These decisions are therefore arguments to say that it is possible for an employee of a public authority to enjoy Convention Rights even though it is a 'private' relationship and similar provisions could not be imposed on private organisations.

4.12 Article 12 Right to marry and found a family

Men and women of marriageable age have the right to marry and to found a family, according to the national laws governing the exercise of this right.

4.12.1 The proviso to this Article is interesting as it has provided the ECtHR with the excuse to leave questions of marriage and family to individual states and, unusually, has not been prepared to offer a broad interpretation of the Article's impact. It provides the right to be able to remarry [*F v Switzerland* (1987) 10 EHRR 411] although, as long as the state makes alternative provision, the prohibition on remarriage imposed by, say, a church does not constitute an infringement of this right.

4.12.2 As stated, however, the right has been narrowly interpreted and does not confer a right to obtain a divorce [*Johnston v Ireland* (1986) 9 EHRR 203], nor does it require a state to treat a stable relationship in the same way as marriage with the same consequences and benefits [*Marckx v Belgium* (1979) 2 EHRR 330].

4.12.3 Previously the ECtHR interpreted the right to marry to mean marriage between members of opposite biological sex [*Rees v United Kingdom* (1986) 9 EHRR 56], thus states did not have to allow same sex marriages nor did they have to allow transsexuals to marry persons who were of the same sex at birth [see for domestic decisions which followed this line of argument, *R v Registrar of Births, Marriages and Deaths ex p Ryder* [2002] EWHC 1191 (Admin) and *R v Ashworth Hospital Authority ex p E* [2001] EWHC Admin 1089]. However, as a demonstration of how the Convention should be seen as an evolving document, the ECtHR very recently [see *Goodwin v United Kingdom*, Times, 12 July 2002] has changed its approach and found that a prohibition on a transsexual marrying a person of his or her same original sex was a violation of Article 12. The ECtHR considered that no substantial hardship or detriment to the public interest would be likely to flow from the recognition of the change of status of transsexuals and so a ban on their ability to marry was no longer sustainable.

4.12.4 The Article can apply to adoption and artificial insemination, although courts will probably grant a high degree of judicial deference to the relevant public authorities in this area.

4.13 Article 14 Freedom from discrimination in respect of Convention Rights

The enjoyment of the rights and freedoms set forth in this Convention shall be secured without discrimination on any ground such as sex, race, colour, language, religion, political or other opinion, national or social origin, association with a national minority, property, birth or other status.

4.13.1 Contrary to some misconceptions, Article 14 does not provide a general freedom from discrimination. The Article does not stand alone and thus to succeed in a challenge, a claimant would need to show that they had been discriminated against in their enjoyment of another Convention Right. They do not need to show a breach of the other Convention Right, otherwise Article 14 would serve no purpose, but they must show that that other Convention right is somehow in play. The measures complained of must be 'linked to the exercise of the right guaranteed' [*Schmidt and Dahlstrom v Sweden* (1976) 1 EHRR 632]. In some ways, therefore, the UK's domestic discrimination laws may provide greater protection than the 1998 Act.

4.13.2   However, first, if a claim under Article 14 can be attached to another Convention Right, it should be noted that the types of discrimination are far wider under Article 14. The types of discrimination listed are not exhaustive but indicative. Thus other types of discrimination, possibly age, for example, might be covered. Second, even where UK law provides protection for discrimination, the coverage of the national legislation may be limited. Thus, for example, the meaning of sex discrimination under the Sex Discrimination Act 1975 does not currently include discrimination on the grounds of sexual orientation [see *Pearce v Governing Body of Mayfield School* [2001] IRLR 669]. Although this will have to change as result of EU directives, it is arguable that Article 14 would also outlaw such discrimination already.

4.13.3   The concept of discrimination within the Article is not dissimilar to that applied domestically in the Sex Discrimination Act 1975, Race Relations Act 1976 and Disability Discrimination Act 1995. The claimant will therefore need to show that he or she has been treated differently or, in UK terms, 'less favourably', than another comparable person on a ground outlawed by the Article. Such treatment will not, however, be unlawful if the state or public authority can show that there is objective and reasonable justification for the difference in treatment, it pursues a legitimate aim and that there is 'a reasonable relationship of proportionality between the means employed and the aim sought to be realised' [*The Belgian Linguistics Case* (1979-80) 1 EHRR 252].

4.14   Article 1 of the First Protocol – Right to property

Every natural or legal person is entitled to the peaceful enjoyment of his possessions. No one shall be deprived of his possessions except in the public interest and subject to the conditions provided for by law and by the general principles of international law.

The preceding provisions shall not, however, in any way impair the right of a State to enforce such laws as it deems necessary to control the use of property in accordance with the general interest or to secure the payment of taxes or other contributions or penalties.

4.14.1 Property, which this qualified right protects, has been defined widely to include: intangible as well as tangible property, in particular intellectual property rights; goodwill in a business; the entitlement to a pension; as well as the more obvious commercial property such as shares and real property. The property must, however, be in the possession of the claimant; an expectation of possession, for example, under a will where the testator is still alive, will not count.

4.14.2 The ECtHR [*Sporrong and Lonnroth v* Sweden (1982) 5 EHRR 35] has held that the right comprises three aspects: first, the peaceful enjoyment of property; second, deprivation of possessions subject to the expressed qualifications; and, third, a recognition that the use of property can be controlled in pursuance of the general interest.

4.14.3 Peaceful enjoyment prevents both actual taking by the state but also action short of confiscation, which interferes with a person's property. This is of particular importance in the environmental field where the Article can be used to support a challenge based on negative environmental impact from a nearby public owned property i.e. potential or actual pollution or blight effect brought about by particular developments.

4.14.4 Deprivation of property applies to actual deprivation, i.e. removal of property from the individual, but also to practical, though not actual, removal, i.e. an individual may still retain possession of an item of property but restrictions or conditions imposed on that possession by a public authority are such as to mean that the individual has been effectively deprived of the asset [*Sporrong and Lonnroth v Sweden* (1982) 5 EHRR 35].

4.14.5 The third aspect, legitimate control, would permit, for example, proper planning controls or property taxation [see, for example, *Pine Valley Developments v Ireland* (1991) 14 EHRR 319 and *Mellacher v Austria* (1989) 12 EHRR 391].

4.14.6 The important qualification permitting interference under this Article is that the 'deprivation' or 'control' must be in the public or general interest and proportionate [*Sporrong and Lonnroth v Sweden* (1982) 5 EHRR 35]. Usually, compensation from the 'taking' public authority will be required and the ECtHR has normally sought to ensure that procedural safeguards to regulate the public authorities' actions are in place.

4.15 Article 2 of the First Protocol – Right to education

4.15.1 Detailed consideration of this Convention Right can be found in the next chapter, Chapter 5.

4.16 Article 3 of the First Protocol – Right to free elections

The High Contracting Parties undertake to hold free elections at reasonable intervals by secret ballot, under conditions which will ensure the free expression of the opinion of the people in the choice of the legislature

4.16.1 Another obvious fundamental right in the preservation of democracy, it was somewhat surprising that this right was not included in the original Convention but had to wait until the First Protocol. However, it applies only to elections to 'the legislature' and does not therefore apply to the majority of elections. It will apply to elections to the House of Commons and the House of Lords, if ever that is directly elected, and will also apply to bodies which have the independent power to issue decrees. It will therefore apply to elections to the devolved assemblies in Scotland, Wales and Northern Ireland and, if ever regional Government with devolved powers appears in England, to elections to regional assemblies too. It is unlikely, however, to apply to elections of local authorities as, despite their bye-law making powers, today's castrated local Government can hardly be described as legislatures, even less so parent governor representatives or school governing bodies.

4.16.2 As indicated above, this brief look at the Convention Rights has omitted any consideration of Article 2 of the First Protocol, the right to education. In a work on education, though, it is appropriate that it should be given detailed scrutiny and therefore we now move to look at this, in theory, important, though, in practice, less so, right in the next chapter.

5. The Right to Education – Article 2 of the First Protocol to the Convention

5.1 Generally

5.1.1　As the right contained in Article 2 of the First Protocol to the Convention is expressed in terms of the right to education, it is perhaps appropriate in a text on the Human Rights Act's effect on education to spend time considering its application. This chapter is therefore devoted to an analysis of the Article and the case law on its effect.

5.1.2　Although on its face the right could be anticipated to have a significant impact on the work of schools and LEAs, this Article's effect has, in fact, so far been fairly limited and, indeed, other articles may have or might in the future have a more important impact on the field of education.

5.1.3　Nonetheless, the Article is still an important part of the Convention and the right was secured as part of the First Protocol signed by the UK on 20 March 1952.

5.1.4　Article 2 of the First Protocol states:

> *'No person shall be denied the right to education. In the exercise of any functions which it assumes in relation to education and to teaching, the state shall respect the right of parents to ensure such education and teaching in conformity with their own religious and philosophical convictions.'*

5.1.5　The Article, however, has been subject to reservations and caveats by a number of countries and, as far as the UK is concerned, the Article must be read subject to the reservation secured at the time the Protocol was signed. This accordingly provides that the principle in the second sentence applies: '*only so far as it is compatible with the provision of efficient instruction and training and the avoidance of unreasonable public expenditure.*'

5.1.6　In other words, the UK Government obtained an 'opt out', the meaning of which will be well known or, at least, the obscurity of the meaning of which will be familiar to practitioners used to discerning the implications of s 9 of the Education Act 1996 or its predecessors dating back to the Education Act 1944 [and see, for example, *Oxfordshire County Council v GB and Others* [2001] EWCA Civ 1358; (2002) LGR 279, CA].

5.1.7 Irrespective of the restrictions, the original article is still also significantly different from the equivalent provision in the Universal Declaration of Human Rights, Article 26(2) of which states:

> *Education shall be directed to the full development of the human personality and to the strengthening of respect for human rights and fundamental freedoms. It shall promote understanding, tolerance and friendship among all nations, racial or religious groups, and shall partner the activities of the United Nations for the maintenance of peace.'*

5.1.8 Article 26(3) of the Universal Declaration adds: '**parents have a prior right to choose the kind of education that shall be given to their children.**'

5.1.9 The possibly utopian ambition of the Universal Declaration might therefore not have been achieved, but Article 2 does nonetheless establish certain, qualified, rights.

5.1.10 As can be seen, as opposed to the Universal Declaration, Article 2 does not prescribe the content or purpose of the education and teaching to be provided. It would not therefore be violated by the inclusion or exclusion of a particular subject on the National Curriculum, unless the subject's omission or addition were to be so serious as to preclude the provision of proper education. States are given a wide discretion to administer and finance their own systems of education [see *SP v United Kingdom* 17 Jan 1997, unreported].

5.1.11 Although Article 2 should be read as a whole, it does comprise two principles, the first of which is dominant, i.e. the right not to be denied education, the second sentence being an adjunct to that first, fundamental right. However, it should also be noticed that the two principles apply to two different potential victims. The first principle applies to any person, which means that the right not to be denied education is, of course, not limited simply to children or young persons; it applies to anyone irrespective of age. The second principle, however, can on its face be invoked only by parents. Again there is no age limit and so, conceivably, it could apply to the parents of anyone, however old they are – a fact that might assist adults with learning difficulties who rely on their parents throughout their life for support, but it is usually used

5.
RIGHT TO
EDUCATION

by parents of school aged children and the right attaches to the parent, not the child. It may be a moot point, but it would seem that the child whose parents' convictions have been abused or ignored could not bring a claim; only the parents.

5.2 The right not to be denied education

5.2.1 The first principle, in fact, comprises four interrelated but separate rights (all of which are qualified or limited – see *The Belgian Linguistics Case* [(1979-80) 1 EHRR 252]):

1. a right of access to such educational establishments as exist at a given time;

2. a right to an effective (but not the most effective possible) education;

3. a right to official recognition of academic qualifications; and

4. a right, when read with the freedom from discrimination guaranteed by Article 14 of the Convention, not to be disadvantaged in the provision of education on any ground such as sex, race, colour, language, religion, political or other opinion, national or social origin, association with a national minority, property, birth or other status without reasonable and objective justification.

A right of access to such educational establishments as exist at a given time

5.2.2 This does not require a state to establish at their own expense or to subsidise education of any particular type at any particular level [*The Belgian Linguistics Case* supra; *X v United Kingdom* (1978) 14 DR 234]. Parents have no right to insist on the provision of single-sex or selective schools. In *W & DM and M & HI v United Kingdom* [[1984] 37 DR 96], the applicants' children were refused places at selective grammar schools. Because the admission quota could not be exceeded without prejudicing efficient education and the efficient use of resources, they had to go to non-selective comprehensives. The complaint was held inadmissible because there was no interference with the parents' role in education nor was there a lack of pluralism, which the ECtHR considered was a primary objective of this Convention Right.

5.2.3 States are not required to recognise or continue to recognise any particular institution as an educational establishment [*Church of X v United Kingdom* 12 YB 306 (1969)]. Similarly, states were not (and it would now follow, domestic public authorities are not) prevented from imposing entry requirements for access to an educational establishment [*X v United Kingdom* 23 DR 228 (1980)]. This case concerned entry requirements on courses of higher education, but would also apply to selection requirements for entry to maintained secondary school or independent schools. Entry requirements based on ability to pay, i.e. access to fee paying independent schools, is also not prohibited but there can be no obligation imposed on a state (or an LEA) to fund private or independent schools, as long as this does not lead to unjustifiable discrimination [*W and KL v Sweden* 45 DR 143 (1985)].

5.2.4   The Article applies to both elementary and secondary education [*X v United Kingdom* 2 DR 50 (1975)] (although other decisions, especially *Foreign Students v United Kingdom* [9 DR 185 (1977)] suggest that Article 2 was concerned primarily with elementary education, i.e. between the ages of 5 and 13). The more accepted view is that the right not to be denied education could apply to a person of any age, although there is no unfettered right to further or higher education according to the European Commission in *X v United Kingdom* [2 DR 50 (1975)].

5.2.5   The right not to be denied education does not prevent pupils or students being excluded from enjoying education for disciplinary reasons. In *Sulak v Turkey* [84-A DR 98 (1996)] a university student had been expelled for cheating repeatedly in examinations. His claim for breach of Article 2 was held inadmissible, even though his expulsion meant he was unable to gain admission to any other university. Applying similar principles to school based education, it would appear that there is no breach in principle in excluding a child, provided, of course, that the proper procedures have been followed and that the exclusion has been in accordance with domestic law.

A right to an effective (but not the most effective possible) education

5.2.6   Although in an echo of English case law [see, for example, *R v Surrey Education Committee ex p H* [(1983) unreported] – there is no obligation on an LEA to provide a utopian system of education] the education made available does not have to be the *most* effective, as long as it is effective, this principle does nonetheless impose a requirement on the public body to provide education of a minimum standard [*The Belgian Linguistics Case*]. Plurality is also a fundamental requirement, so that the curriculum should not seek to pursue one tenet or belief and, in the same way, teaching staff should not attempt to indoctrinate children [*Kjeldsen, Busk Madsen and Pedersen v Denmark* (1976) 1 EHRR 711]. Effective education may be relevant in the context of immigration cases. For example, in *Holub and Holub v Secretary of State for the Home Department* [[2001] ELR 401, CA] the Court of Appeal declined a decision to return the applicants to Poland. They had argued that because of, in their view, the inferior system of education in Poland, their daughter would be deprived of an effective education if forced to return to the country of her nationality. The Court of Appeal held that this element of the Article 2 of the First Protocol could not be invoked simply because the applicants' daughter would receive a better education in the United Kingdom. They found that Poland had a well-developed system of education and that therefore the daughter would not be denied an effective education if returned there. The implication, however, might be drawn that if a state to which a person was to be returned had no well-developed system of education or none at all, then the right to an effective education might be used to resist a child's return to such a country. Fortunately though, that is a matter which can be left to immigration lawyers.

A right to official recognition of academic qualifications

5.2.7 Again, this principle is partly to preserve plurality [see, for example, *Kjeldsen, Busk Madsen and Pedersen v Denmark* (1976) 1 EHRR 711] and *In the Petition of Dove and Dove for judicial review of the acts of Scottish Ministers in relation to St Mary's Episcopal Primary School, Dunblane* 31 July 2002, unreported] and to ensure that certain educational institutes which propound particular views do not enjoy a monopoly. It does not mean, however, that all qualifications have to be recognised. Properly imposed requirements to ensure academic qualifications meet certain reasonable standards should not fall foul of this principle.

A right, when read with the freedom from discrimination guaranteed by Article 14 of the Convention, not to be disadvantaged in the provision of education on any ground such as sex, race, colour, language, religion, political or other opinion, national or social origin, association with a national minority, property, birth or other status without reasonable and objective justification

5.2.8 This principle arises, in effect, from the combination of Article 14 and Article 2 of the First Protocol. UK law has previously enacted legislation to prohibit race and sex discrimination and, from 1 September 2002, has addressed disability discrimination in education. Cases based on other types of discrimination (for example, age and sexual orientation discrimination) may be brought, but the effect of this sub-right is likely to be limited in light of the leading case, *The Belgian Linguistics Case*[(1979-80) 1 EHRR 252].

5.2.9 In this case, French speaking Belgian parents living in a Dutch speaking area of Belgium wanted their children to be educated in French and complained that under Belgian law their French-speaking children were unable to be educated in the French language since they lived in a Dutch-speaking part of Belgium where the schooling was conducted in Dutch. The ECtHR held that the first sentence of Article 2 does not require that states establish an educational system or subsidise a particular type or level of educational system: 'The Convention lays down no specific obligations concerning the extent of these means and the manner of their organisation or subsidisation.' Instead, the obligation on the state was to guarantee individuals the 'right of access to educational institutions existing at the time' and that the State should regulate education which 'may vary in time and place according to the needs and resources of the community and of individuals'. For that right to be effective it was necessary that the individual should be able to have official recognition of studies which he or she had completed. Further, the right was 'meaningless if it did not imply, in favour of the beneficiaries, the right to be educated in the national language or in one of the national languages'. However, the Court stated that the first sentence of Article 2 of the First Protocol did not specify the language in which education must be conducted in order that the right is protected. As for the second limb of Article 2, the ECtHR held that it did not guarantee a right to education nor did it require respect for parents' linguistic preferences, but only their religious and philosophical convictions. The object of the second sentence of Article 2 was not to secure respect of a right for parents to have education conducted in a language other than that of the country in question.

5.3 Respect for the religious and philosophical convictions of parents

5.3.1 The second, allegedly subsidiary, limb of Article 2 of the First Protocol is the obligation on the state/ public authority in the exercise of any functions which it assumes in relation to education and teaching to respect the right of parents to ensure such education and teaching in conformity with their own religious and philosophical convictions.

5.3.2 The first point to notice is that this grants the right to the parent not to the child so, in effect, the child's own religious and philosophical convictions carry subsidiary weight (if any). ECtHR case law does, however, conflict with UK law in the interpretation given to the meaning of 'parent'. The meaning is consistent with the Children Act 1989 so far as children in care are concerned, i.e. the child's natural parents can still exercise Article 2 rights [*Aminoff v Sweden* 43 DR 120 (1985)], but in contrast to UK law, the ECtHR has held that if one parent gains custody of a child, the other parent loses their right [*X v Sweden* 12 DR 192 (1977)]. Although the potential number of persons who can be regarded as having parental responsibility or being classed as parents in UK law is wide, it is suggested that domestic courts will disregard the ECtHR precedents here and will permit those persons who are parents under s 576 of the EA 1996 to exercise Article 2 rights. In particular, this would mean that a parent who does not have custody would still be entitled to have their religious and/or philosophical convictions respected.

5.3.3   From the ECtHR case law, the right applies to both public and private education so far as state protection is concerned [see *Campbell and Cosans v United Kingdom*], although for LEA purposes, convictions in the context of private education are likely only to arise where a) an LEA is seeking to place a child in a non-maintained or independent school [but now see *CB v Merton LBC and SENT* [2002] EWHC 877 (Admin), [2002] ELR 441] or b) the parent is putting forward an argument about the respective merits of public and private education. The latter argument is, however, unlikely to establish a breach of the Convention Right as the right does not extend to requiring a public authority to provide private education if the parent objects to education in the state sector. The key, again, is plurality. As long as parents have the choice of provision, and even if that choice is limited because they cannot afford to pay certain schools' fees, nonetheless, there will not be an infringement of this right [see *R v Department for Education and Employment ex parte Begbie* [1999] ELR, QBD].

5.3.4   What is or is not a 'conviction' is clearly important. It is not sufficient for a parent to think that something is a good idea or to have an opinion on the issue. A 'conviction' is more in the nature of a belief which must 'attain a certain level of cogency, seriousness, cohesion and importance'. The onus of establishing the conviction lies with the parents (despite the comments of three judges in *Valsamis* who argued that the parent's conviction should be accepted unless it is unfounded and/or unreasonable) and it must be genuinely held. Ordinarily (and after the 1998 Act it will happen), the parents should raise their objection with the school or LEA or Secretary of State before issuing proceedings in the ECtHR [see *Warwick v United Kingdom* 60 DR 5 (1989)] and, it would follow, that national courts and tribunals will wish to see if parents have exhausted their rights to complain to these organisations first.

5.3.5   Although there is little in the way of case law, it would appear that the convictions which may be protected are limited. For example, a belief that their child should be taught in a particular language was not a conviction which was protected by Article 2 (*The Belgian Linguistics Case*). What may be a religious conviction is possibly easier to identify; the same principles will apply as in the case of the freedom of religion, Article 9 [see Chapter 4 above]. Philosophical convictions may be harder to identify but will comprise such convictions 'as are worthy of respect in a "democratic society"…and are not incompatible with human dignity; in addition, they must not conflict with the fundamental right of the child to education' [*Campbell and Cosans v United Kingdom* Campbell and Cosans v UK]. A belief that a white child should not attend a school with pupils from other ethnic backgrounds should not amount to a conviction worthy of protection, but a belief in home educating on educational grounds may well do. Although, if the child receives no education as a result and the parents' belief in home educating is simply a ruse to condone the child's truanting, a court may take a different view. Of particular relevance are two recent High Court decisions. In the first, *Williamson v Secretary of State for Education and Employment* [[2001] EWHC Admin 960 (Admin); [2002] EWCA Civ 1820], Elias J and subsequently the Court of Appeal held that an objection to the fact that schools could not administer corporal punishment was not a philosophical conviction. This was distinguished from the fact that objections to the administration of corporal punishment had been considered philosophical convictions by the ECtHR [see *Campbell and Cosans v United Kingdom* (1982) 4 EHRR 293] because the law had always shown a respect for an individual's physical integrity (although not expressly stated, the judge was perhaps recognising that the children's Article 8 rights had to be balanced) and stronger reason was required to justify the right to inflict physical injury than was required to prevent its infliction. In the second, *T v SENT and Wiltshire County Council* [[2002] EWHC 1474 (Admin)] Richards J held that the parents' views that their child should receive Lovaas provision[1] was not a philosophical conviction. Their views were, the judge accepted, based on a judgement that such a programme would be more likely to meet their child's educational needs and enable him to be integrated into mainstream schooling. But that, he held, fell far short of a philosophical conviction in favour of the Lovaas programme. His judgment also suggests that parental views as to the appropriate form of most, if not all, educational provision for their child are unlikely to amount to philosophical convictions.

5.3.6   In Article 2, religion and philosophical convictions are joined by 'and'. It is, however, suggested that the two are distinct, indeed can be mutually incompatible in certain cases. Thus, a parent need not show that their conviction is both a religious *and* philosophical one, simply that it is either a religious conviction and/or a philosophical one.

5.3.7   The obligation to respect a parent's convictions is also unclear. 'Respect' means more than take into account, but does not provide the parent with the right of veto or a mandatory power over the public authority. Maybe the Ali G concept of 'Respec' is nearer the mark. The conviction must

---

[1]   The Lovaas approach offers early intensive behaviour modification therapy to children with autism and related disorders. The home based programme consists of 40 hours a week of structured input, ideally from the age of three, delivered by specially trained students.

be considered, given due weight, and valued, but not necessarily be followed if there are valid reasons for not doing so. Considerable discretion has been given to states as to how they should or can respect a parent's convictions, unless, of course, there is only one way in which they can be lawfully valued [*Campbell and Cosans v United Kingdom* (1982) 4 EHRR 293]. Some light on this aspect of the Convention Right has, however, been cast by Collins J in *R (on the application of K) v Newham LBC* [2002] EWHC 405 (Admin). The substance of the case is considered in Chapter 6, but the court held that a devout Muslim parent's desire on religious grounds that his daughter should attend a single sex school so that she did not mix with boys or young men, was a religious conviction. What that meant was that, in that case, the LEA as admissions authority, had to give due weight to that conviction and, to enable them to do this, their admission forms had to provide a space to enable parents to record their convictions and that the importance of religious (and, it follows, philosophical convictions) should be drawn to their attention. Thus it seems 'due weight' must be given if a valid conviction is raised, but that need not be taken as either a veto or a factor which compels the authority to do something if valid circumstances outweigh the conviction.

5.4 Dove and Dove

5.4.1 All these principles, drawn mainly from the case law of the ECtHR and Commission, have been analysed and applied in the important decision of the Court of Session in *Dove and Dove* [*In the Petition of Dove and Dove for judicial review of the acts of Scottish Ministers in relation to St Mary's Episcopal Primary School, Dunblane* 31 July 2002, unreported]. Although this was a Scottish case, the views expressed by Lord Cameron in his leading judgment are likely to be applied in the English courts.

5.4.2 In *Dove*, parents of a pupil at St Mary's Episcopal Primary School, Dunblane, sought judicial review of the decision of the Scottish Office to end self-governing status for the school and transferring the management of the school to an education authority with its future funding coming directly from the authority. This was apparently a different fate to the only other self-governing school in Scotland, which was continuing to exist outside education authority control. The parents also challenged the decision of the Scottish Office to refuse grant aid to the school because it had decided to end its self-governing status.

5.4.3 The parents based their case on Article 2 of the First Protocol and, in part, its combination with Article 14 arguing that:

1.   the decisions had deprived their son of his right to education, in that the proposed changes in the method of managing the school had the potential to change the character and nature of the school and thus had consequences for the effectiveness of the education provided for pupils in the school;

2.   that the decisions conflicted with the parents' own philosophical convictions, i.e. that they did not want their child educated in a school maintained by an LEA; and

3.   that by treating this school differently from the other self-governing school there was discrimination contrary to Article 14.

5.4.4   Lord Cameron reviewed the ECtHR and Commission judgments on the right to education and noted that an attack on the comprehensive system had been rejected [*W and DM v United Kingdom* [1984] 37 DR 96]. He also noted the Scottish Office's argument that in the *travaux préparatoires* concerning what ultimately became Article 2, it was clear that the aim of the Article was to secure that in each of the Contracting States the system of education was free from totalitarianism. This was made plain by the Court in *Kjeldsen*. In relation to the second sentence of the Article, the convictions of parents did not require to be reflected but only respected.

5.
RIGHT TO
EDUCATION

5.4.5   His conclusion was [at paragraph 16] that:

'The general right to education in the first sentence of Article 2, it has been said, dominates the article. For that reason, any interpretation given to the right of parents to have philosophical convictions taken into account must not conflict with the primary right to education enjoyed by the child. See *Campbell and Cosans* at paragraph 36. Incorporated within that general right are the four separate rights (none of which is absolute) namely, a right of access to such educational establishments as exist; a right to effective (but not the most effective possible) education, a right to official recognition of academic qualifications and a right, when read with the freedom from discrimination guaranteed by Article 14 of the Convention, not to be disadvantaged in the provision of education on any ground such as sex, race, colour, language, religion, political or other opinion, national or social origin, association with a national minority, property, birth or other status without reasonable and objective justification. The state is entitled to regulate these rights, taking account of individual and community needs and resources, provided this does not injure the substance of the right to education nor conflict with other rights enshrined in the Convention — see *The Belgian Linguistic Case.*'

5.4.6　*The Belgian Linguistics case*, he pointed out, had not required each state to establish a general and official educational system:

> '... but merely of guaranteeing to persons subject to the jurisdiction of the Contracting parties the right, in principle, to avail themselves of the means of instruction existing at a given time... Persons subject to the jurisdiction of a Contracting State cannot draw from Article 2 of the First Protocol the right to obtain from the public authorities the creation of a particular kind of educational establishment; nevertheless, a state which had set up such an establishment could not, in laying down entrance requirements, take discriminatory measures within the meaning of Article 14.'

5.4.7　Lord Cameron concluded [at paragraph 26]

> 'It follows that measures such as the orders and directions complained of in this petition which are concerned only with regulation of the constitution of the management and control of the management and administration of a school and which do not affect the curricula or teaching at the school, that is to say, the effectiveness of the education offered there, or limit access to the school or the education offered at it, do not fall within the scope or ambit of the right to education guaranteed by the first sentence of Article 2. They do not constitute a disadvantage to any of the modalities of the exercise of that right nor are they linked to the exercise of that right.'

5.4.8　The Court of Session concluded that a refusal of grant-aided status could not by itself constitute any disadvantage to the exercise by the parents' son of any of the modalities of the exercise of that right nor could it be linked to any discrimination in the exercise of the right by way of access to education. That therefore disposed of the claim that the first sentence of Article 2 had been infringed.

5.4.9　Turning to the second sentence, the Court held that the parents' belief that the school's management before it was returned to education authority control was to the significant educational advantage of their child was not a religious or philosophical conviction within the meaning of that phrase in Article 2 of the First Protocol. Citing the ECtHR's decision in *Valsamis v Greece*, Lord Cameron noted [at paragraph 29] that the word 'convictions', taken on its own, is not synonymous with the words 'opinions' and 'ideas'. It denotes views that attain a certain level of cogency, seriousness, cohesion and importance. It was also pointed out that the second sentence of Article 2 of the First Protocol relates to the content of the education provided for a child, not to the administrative arrangements for its provision [at paragraph 33]. Covering all eventualities, the Court then held that even if the parents' beliefs amounted to philosophical convictions, so long as the plurality of the education system was protected, there would be no infringement in any event. '[E]ven if it were to be the case that the [parents'] beliefs were to amount to philosophical convictions such that the Scottish Ministers were obliged to have respect for them, then, as was pointed out in *Kjeldsen*, there is within the system of education in this country the opportunity for the [parents], in the name of their creed or opinions, to dissociate their child from St. Mary's as a local authority controlled school and entrust him to a private and independently governed school.'

5.4.10   Finally, the Court of Session considered the claim that there had been unlawful discrimination under Article 14, when combined with Article 2 of the First Protocol. They found that it was unfounded. Referring to *Kjeldsen, Busk, Madsen and Petersen v Sweden* [(1976) Series A No 23] they endorsed the ECtHR's view that 'Article 14 prohibits, within the ambit of the rights and freedoms guaranteed, discriminatory treatment having as its basis or reason a personal characteristic ("status") by which persons or groups of persons are distinguishable from each other'. That being the guiding principle, Lord Cameron concluded that 'Examination of the legislation and the matters complained of by the [parents] does not indicate that they distinguish [themselves] and other parents at St. Mary's from other parents in the education system, including those with children at [the other self-governing school], by virtue of their status as a group with philosophical convictions…In the present case there is nothing to which the [parents] point which indicates that upon transfer of management there will be any difference in treatment in curricular matters, teaching or funding, between the present situation as it affects both St. Mary's and [the other self-governing school] (even assuming that the latter can be considered as a State school) and the situation which would obtain after a transfer of management at St Mary's to the local authority.' In so finding, the Court dismissed the claim of discrimination. In addition, the Court indicated that it was prepared to grant public authorities a wide element of deference in this area in terms both of setting and planning the curriculum, but also in the methodology of management to be applied in the state sector [at paragraph 32].

6. School Organisation, the Provision of School Places and Admissions

6.1 Introduction

6.1.1 Initially, concerns were expressed that the Human Rights Act would have an effect on the planning of school places and, most particularly, the provision of school places for individual children. Some felt that if Article 2 of the First Protocol promised a right to education, it could also give parents a right to choose a school, something promised by default in the old Parents' Charter of the early 1990s but never forthcoming in law. This was mainly based on the view that the right to education would create greater obligations on LEAs.

6.1.2 In practice, with a couple of exceptions, the 1998 Act has so far had little impact on the organisation of schooling, admission policies and decisions or admission appeals.

6.2 The provision of school places

6.2.1 All LEAs are under a duty to secure sufficient schools for providing primary and secondary education within their areas [s 14 EA 1996]. However, LEAs need not provide sufficient schools themselves; although in the majority of cases they are the providers of most schools, they can discharge their duty by ensuring that there are sufficient places for their school-aged population in maintained, but also independent, schools, including academies and city technology colleges.

6.2.2 The Article 2 of the First Protocol right to education therefore adds little to what is already a domestic statutory duty, albeit one which is a target duty rather than one imposing strict obligations to provide places at all times [see *R v ILEA ex p Ali* [1990] COD 317].

6.2.3 As has been seen, Article 2 of the First Protocol is considered to have been aimed primarily at ensuring plurality in a state education system. It is worded in the sense of preventing a public authority denying education to a person, rather than a positive obligation to provide it, let alone provide it in a particular type of school or in a particular school.

6.2.4   Nonetheless, LEAs are frequently accused of failing to provide sufficient school places in a particular area. In reality, the complaint is usually not that there are insufficient school places, but that there are insufficient school places in the schools parents want their children to attend. Although, the point has not yet been tested, as long as the LEA has ensured that provision is available within a reasonable distance of the parental home, even if the parents were unhappy with the proposed placement, it is unlikely that the LEA would be infringing the child's right to education.

6.2.5   This does, though, suggest arguments over what may be a reasonable distance. This may cause problems for large LEAs – is it enough to provide sufficient places throughout its area even if its area may be vast? Section 14 suggests that this would be sufficient. The logic might however be challenged if an LEA were to say to a parent that, whilst there are no places for their child within ten miles of their home, they could find one within 50 miles and thereby meet their duty. In contrast, in the case of smaller LEAs, where a small LEA cannot make provision, does it meet its target duty and ensure no infringement with the right to education if it ensures that sufficient places are available taking into account spaces in schools maintained by neighbouring LEAs?

6.2.6   Whilst, however, the right to education may support or supplement an LEA's duty to secure sufficient schools, it does not oblige LEAs to provide schools of a particular nature or a particular ethos. Thus, the Convention Right cannot be used by, for example, minority faiths or religions to require the establishment of voluntary aided schools for their particular faith or religion; nor will it require schools to be established to meet the philosophical convictions of sets of parents; nor does it require schools to be established to teach in particular languages, the most evident example being Welsh speaking schools in Wales.

6.2.7   This conclusion can be drawn in a number of the Commission's and ECtHR's decisions from *The Belgian Linguistics Case* through to the recent judgment of the Scottish Court of Sessions in *Dove* [unreported 31 July 2002 and see Chapter 5].

6.2.8   In *The Belgian Linguistics Case*, the parents, in effect, argued that Article 2 of the First Protocol enabled them to compel the state to establish a school to meet their particular convictions, in their case, a belief that their children should be taught in a French-speaking school in an area of Belgium where schools were Dutch speaking. The ECtHR held that Article 2 of the First Protocol did not require a state or, now, a public authority to establish at their own expense, or to subsidise, education of any particular type at any particular level. Instead, the right to education meant that public authorities were required to guarantee individuals the right of access to educational institutions existing at the time.

6.2.9   Similarly, public authorities are not required to recognise any particular institution as an educational establishment [*Church of X v United Kingdom* 12 YB 306 (1969)] nor to provide single-sex schools, especially where parents are adamant that their children should receive such education, for religious or philosophical reasons [see *R (on the application of K) v Newham LBC* [2002] EWHC 405 (Admin)]. Nor can a public authority be required either to provide selective education or, conversely, to provide solely non-selective education [*W & DM and M & HI v United Kingdom* [1984] 37 DR 96].

6.2.10   School organisation and reorganisation, as opposed to school provision, is heavily regulated and is unlikely to raise any Human Rights Act issues provided, as stated above, no child is denied education as a consequence.

6.2.11   What though if parents are opposed to the reorganisation (often involving a school closure) or they feel that they are prevented from expressing their views or what they may claim to be convictions?

6.2.12   In *Buchan for judicial review of a decision of the Education Services Committee of West Lothian Council* [[2001] ScotCS 175], the court held the derogation to Article 2 of the First Protocol permitted education authorities to make certain decisions based upon efficient instruction and training and the avoidance of unreasonable expenditure. On the facts, it concluded that the decision of the Council in that case to close a school fell within those derogations. This suggests that so long as any school closure is based upon arguments relating to efficient instruction and training or the avoidance of unreasonable expenditure (for example, removing surplus school places) it should be safe from challenge under Article 2 of the First Protocol.

6.2.13   *Dove* [unreported 31 July 2002], albeit also a Scottish case, does address the effect of the Human Rights Act on school reorganisation even more substantially, although it should be remembered that the parents in that case were held not to have a religious or philosophical conviction. The view which formed the basis of the parents' action was that they wanted their child to be educated in a self-governing school. The Court of Session held [at paragraph 33] that the convictions had to relate to the content of education provided for a child, not to the administrative arrangements for its provision.

6.2.14 If a reorganisation were to interfere with actual religious or philosophical convictions, the decision might be somewhat different, but it is hard to imagine where such a possibility might arise other than in an extreme case of, say, a reorganisation which attempts to close a denominational school without alternative denominational provision being available within the LEA's area.

6.2.15 On the subject of reorganisation, it is unlikely that a decision to close a school will determine any civil rights. In *R (on the application of WB and KA) v Leeds School Organisation Committee* [(2002) Times 22 October, Admin] a parents group attempted to challenge a decision of a school organisation committee on the basis that they had been unable to make oral objections. What is interesting about this case, and somewhat unusual given the tendency of some lawyers to throw in Human Rights Act grounds whenever possible, is that no point was taken as to whether or not the SOC had to comply with Article 6 (the right to a fair trial). This must be correct though. The decision of a SOC to, in effect, close a school is not determinative of any individual's civil rights. Certainly not parents, nor even pupils who attend the school - thanks to *Simpson* there is no private civil right to a school place — and even teachers who may lose their jobs as a result of the closure do not have their rights determined by the SOC. That will come later when specific decisions are made relating to their individual contracts of employment.

6. SCHOOL ORGANISATION

6.3 Admissions

6.3.1 As has been highlighted, provided that a child has an opportunity to attend school and one where lessons are taught in the, or one of the, national languages, Article 2 of the First Protocol is unlikely to be infringed. It is therefore even less likely that the Article will be invoked in respect of individual admission policies or decisions.

Admission policies

6.3.2 In formulating admission policies, however, admissions authorities must be aware of the importance of permitting parents to set out their convictions when expressing a preference for a particular school.

6.3.3 In *R (on the application of K) v Newham LBC* [[2002] EWHC 405 (Admin)], the applicants had expressed the preference for their daughter to attend a single sex school. The parents were devout Muslims and were concerned that their daughter should not mix with boys or young men. The application was refused and the parents appealed, arguing that they wished their daughter to benefit from single sex education, although not specifically arguing that this was founded on their religious convictions. The parents' appeal was one of a number heard at the same time, and whilst the appeals of three other parents were successful, this parent's appeal was not and the appeal panel concluded that the parent's reasons did not outweigh the prejudice that would be caused by further admissions. The parents applied for judicial review of that decision. They were successful.

6.3.4   Although maintaining the position that a desire for single-sex education would not in itself amount to a conviction sufficient to engage Article 2(1) of the First Protocol, the court held that the basis for the parents' preference was a religious conviction and that should have been properly considered by the admissions authority and the appeal panel. Collins J commented [at paragraph 29]:

'It seems to me, in those circumstances, that since the coming into effect of the Human Rights Act, the religious conviction of a parent is something to which due weight must be given in considering admission to a particular school. It may be that it is unusual that religious conviction should play a part in a decision whether a single sex or a mixed sex school should be chosen. But there is no question but that in the case of this claimant, and it may be, one suspects, that there are others who will be in the same position, that is an important consideration.'

6.3.5   In his view, certain reasons expressed by parents would not amount to convictions engaging the Convention Right. Thus [at paragraph 37]: '...for example, reasons such as "My daughter would in my view achieve more at a single sex school" or "Single sex schools are better for my child" or any such general reasons for choosing a single sex as opposed to mixed sex, would not and could not overcome or be relevant to the relevant policy.'

6.3.6   However, he considered [at paragraph 38*ff*] that there could be other reasons that would be based on Convention Right convictions, and religious convictions would be one of them, which would mean:

'38 ...in the context of an admission case such as this, that the LEA, initially, and the Appeal Panel on appeal must give weight to such conviction. Indeed, as it seems to me, it is necessary that the LEA and, indeed, all LEAs, take that on board in their admissions policies.

'39. The desirability of enabling children to attend the same school as siblings is already recognised and most, I suspect perhaps all, admissions policies have that as a very important criterion. That is now rendered the more necessary because of the provisions of

Article 8 of the Convention. There should, in my judgment, therefore, be a means of identifying religious conviction. This is something to which attention can be drawn in the relevant pamphlet or guidance note that is issued routinely by the LEA to parents who have to decide where their children should go or where they would like their children to go to receive their secondary education and, indeed, perhaps their primary education as well.

'40. It does not seem to me that for that purpose there needs to be anything special on the form, provided there is a space for the observations and provided that the importance of religious conviction as a reason is drawn to the parents' attention.

'41. But this policy, in addition, as it seems to me, falls down on the failure to identify whether the preference for the single sex school was based on the fact that it was single sex as opposed to any other consideration. I appreciate the evidence given that there were difficulties that arose, or were said to arise, from the need to tick a box on the form indicating whether the choice of a single sex school was on the basis that it was a single sex school, as opposed to any other reason. Nonetheless, as it seems to me, if the criterion is going to be based on a choice of a single sex or a mixed sex school there should be some means of ensuring that the Local Education Authority knows those who have deliberately made that choice because otherwise there will be placed ahead, or may be placed ahead, of those who genuinely have chosen it for that reason, those who have not. This would be unfair to those who have chosen it deliberately for that reason.'

6.3.7 It will therefore be essential for admissions authorities when publishing their policies, but more importantly, the relevant application form, that sufficient opportunity is given for parents to explain *why* they have expressed a particular preference for a particular school. The admission authority will then have to be able to identify which of those reasons stated can amount to religious or philosophical convictions [as to what may amount to a conviction, see 5.3.1*ff* above] and, if they do, give them due weight. The same will apply to admission panels which will have to be able to identify what are and are not legitimate convictions and then ensure that they are taken into account.

6.3.8 Another interesting point from the *Newham* case, which may simply have been a throwaway remark is the assumption that Collins J made about siblings: 'The desirability of enabling children to attend the same school as siblings is already recognised and most, I suspect perhaps all, admissions policies have that as a very important criterion. That is now rendered the more necessary because of the provisions of Article 8 of the Convention.' It presumably did not require any further consideration in the case as the court was concerned with how parents could express their particular circumstances; sibling connections are usually more obvious than a parent's philosophical conviction. Nevertheless, it does raise the important point that an admissions policy which failed to deal with sibling connections could infringe the right to a family life and, on appeal, an appeal panel may well have to consider whether a decision to refuse a child a place at a school which his or her brother or sister attend would be a breach of Article 8. This could be particularly true if, as a consequence of the decision, a parent has to try getting two or more siblings to different schools which might be some distance away when they do not have any transport or public transport is inadequate. Collins J's comments do appear to be at variance with earlier, albeit *obiter*, comments made in two cases, one before and one after the Human Rights Act came into force. In *R v J Roman Catholic Primary School Appeal Panel ex parte O* [2001] ELR 469], Newman J indicated that Article 8 would confer (this was a pre-Human Rights Act decision under challenge) no absolute right to have a child admitted to a school already attended by a sibling. Then in *R v School Admissions Appeals Panel for Hounslow LBC ex parte Hounslow LBC* [[2002] EWCA Civ 900], the Court of Appeal considered that a sibling link did not necessarily have any greater force than any other fair, lawfully adopted criteria in an admissions policy. The impact of Collins J's comments in *Newham* may have to await future decision, but admission appeal panels would be ill-advised to disregard totally an argument that an admission decision which splits siblings may bring Article 8 into play.

6. SCHOOL ORGANISATION

6.4 Admission appeals

6.4.1 Under s 94 of the SSFA 1998, admission authorities are under a duty to make arrangements for enabling the parent of a child to appeal against any decision as to the school at which education is to be provided for the child. Schedule 24 of the SSFA 1998 provides for the membership and constitution of the panels and disqualifies those who have past or present connections with the admissions authority of a kind which might reasonably be taken to raise doubts about their ability to act impartially. Further guidance is given in the Code of Practice on School Admission Appeals [Annex A, paragraph A3]. Nonetheless, it is still the admission authority which appoints. The admission authority can also dismiss or threaten to dismiss members of the panel [see *R (on the application of South Gloucestershire Local Education Authority) v South Gloucestershire Schools Appeal Panel* [2001] EWHC 732 (Admin)] and it is the admissions authority whose decision is challenged before such panels.

6.4.2   This problem was highlighted in the Leggatt Report [*Tribunals for Users: One System One Service* March, 2001, LCD], which reviewed the constitution and work of tribunals. On school admission appeal panels, it said [at page 180, paragraph 12]: 'There are other and more serious such threats to [appeal panels'] independence. First, the appointments are made by the LEA or governing body concerned. Its staff select the panels to hear individual cases. It is the respondent. Whatever steps are taken to keep separate the relevant responsibilities within the authority, users are unlikely to feel that they are assured of true independence.'

6.4.3   If Lord Justice Leggatt was raising concerns about admission appeal panels' independence and impartiality, it was predicted that a parent would sooner or later argue that because of their set up, panels would infringe Article 6 – the right to a fair trial.

6.4.4   That challenge came in the *Alperton* case [*R (on the application of B (through his mother and litigation friend 'VR')) v Head Teacher of Alperton Community School: Governing Body of Alperton Community School: Independent Appeal Committee of Alperton Community School and Secretary of State for Education and Employment* [2001] EWHC Admin 229] at first instance. (There was a subsequent appeal to the Court of Appeal, but only in respect of the exclusion appeals considered in that case. The court's decision on the admission appeal panel aspects of the case was not appealed as, for non-Human Rights Act reasons, it quashed the panel's decision.) As far as the admission appeal was concerned, it was alleged that the provisions of the School Standards and Framework Act 1998 governing admissions appeals created actual or apparent bias or unfairness because the governing body (it was a challenge to a decision of the appeal panel for a voluntary aided school) or LEA (in other cases) appoint, train and pay panel members and they have no security of tenure.

6.4.5   Having considered lengthy arguments, Newman J rejected the submissions that in English law there is a civil right to an education suitable to one's needs. In reaching this conclusion, he relied on the ECtHR case law on Article 6 considered in Chapter 4 and, in particular, *Simpson v United Kingdom* [(1989) 64 DR 188]. Having reached the conclusion Article 6 was inapplicable, the judge nonetheless went on to analyse the independence and impartiality of admission appeal panels [paragraph 71]. 'I can see no threat to impartiality from formal training and nor does payment amounting to compensation for loss suffered as a result of attendance and travelling and subsistence allowances give rise to any realistic prospect of compromise. The statutory framework ensures that persons with a possible interest which might give rise to the appearance of bias are excluded from membership… As to security of tenure, it is but one aspect to be considered…In this instance the members of the independent appeal panel are acting out of public duty. There is no career structure and no remuneration and there is no real risk of them being influenced by factors such as reappointment in the discharge of their duties. They are appointed and deal with individual appeals and they cannot be removed during the currency of appeals.'

6.4.6   Consequently it would appear that admission appeal panels are in general safe from challenge under the Human Rights Act.

6.5   Points specific to key stage 1 or infant class size reduction, admissions and admission appeals

6.5.1   Whether known as key stage 1 or infant class size reduction admissions (for the purposes of this book they will be referred to as 'infant class size'), it was always felt that these special admission arrangements could be perceived as falling foul of some part of the Human Rights Act. Limiting class sizes to 30 clearly restricts the ability of parents to express a preference and, more particularly, disappointed parents of infant children have very reduced rights of appeal.

6.5.2   By virtue of s 1(6) of the SSFA 98 LEAs and governing bodies are required to exercise their functions with a view to securing that the limit imposed by the Secretary of State, specifying the number of pupils that a class to which the limit applies may contain while an ordinary teaching session is conducted by a single qualified teacher, is complied with in relation to that class. That specified number is currently 30 and applies to infant classes of 5, 6 and 7 year olds. [And see the Education (Infant Class Sizes) (Wales) Regulations 1998, S1 1998/1943 and the Education (Infant Class Sizes) (England) Regulations 1998, S1 1998/1973.]

6.5.3   Where a child has been refused admission on the grounds that prejudice to efficient education or the efficient use of resources would arise by reason of the measures required to keep to the statutory class size limit (for example, if the school would have to employ an additional teacher to ensure there were no more then 30 children in a class at any one time), a parent can appeal against the decision to refuse admission. However, the admission appeal panel can allow the appeal and offer a place to the child only where the panel is satisfied either a) that the decision to refuse admission was not one which a reasonable admission authority would have made in the circumstances of the case or b) that an error has been made in the application of the admissions policy and that the child would have been offered a place if the admission arrangements had been properly implemented. This clearly provides parents with less opportunity of success than in the case of appeals for other age groups where the parent needs only to show that the merits of their child's case outweigh any prejudice their child's admission would cause.

6.5.4   As expected, parents have challenged admission appeal panel decisions which have not allowed appeals. This was particularly so where panels felt unable to take account of any personal circumstances because of advice from the DfEE [see *Admissions to infant classes from September 2000* Ref DfEE 0016/2000]. This said in a suggested wording for letters advising parents of the appeal process that 'You are free to talk about personal factors at the appeal hearing if you want, but in this type of appeal the appeal panel cannot take them into account unless they are relevant to one or other of the two things they are allowed to look at [i.e. the two grounds on which an appeal can be allowed]'.

6.5.5   This advice reflected early decisions of the courts in *R v Southend Borough Education Appeals Committee ex parte Southend on Sea Borough Council and others* [unreported - judgment 17 August 1999] and *R v Richmond upon Thames London Borough Council, ex p JC* [[2000] ELR 565 CA]. In the *Southend* case, the judge found it unnecessary to reach any conclusions on the issue but nonetheless expressed a provisional view. '[Ground (a), i.e. a decision no reasonable admissions authority would make] clearly introduces a test of the kind with which this court is familiar, normally referred to as a "Wednesbury unreasonable" test. The Appeal Committee must ask itself under that sub-paragraph whether the decision was one which a reasonable admission authority could make; or, to put it another way, whether it was within the range of responses open to a reasonable admissions authority.' He indicated that the role of the admission panel was more akin to the court in judicial review cases, i.e. it was there to review the decision rather than to consider the merits and substitute its own opinion for that of the admissions authority.

6.5.6   This notion of the panel's role being one simply of review was followed in the *Richmond* case where, again, the court discouraged appeal panels from getting too involved with the facts or merits of a parent's case. 'It seems clear that the guidance envisages that the hearing will be by way of review and in no sense a rehearing, both the exercise of testing the reasonableness of a decision and inquiring whether criteria have been properly applied are classically the province of an appellate authority when reviewing a decision and not of a reconsideration and independent assessment of the position as is to be found when an appeal is by way of rehearing.'

6.5.7   The compatibility of restrictions imposed on infant class size appeals with the Human Rights Act was also tested in the *Richmond upon Thames* case, where the Court of Appeal, albeit in a decision prior to the Human Rights Act coming into force, considered the effect of Article 6 on admission appeals but also in the particular context of infant class size appeals. Whilst recognising that the infant class size provisions deprived parents of certain rights, the Court nonetheless considered that there was no determination of a parent or child's private civil rights so Article 6 did not come into play.

6.5.8   The trend towards review rather than a rehear was followed to a certain extent in the *South Gloucestershire* case [*R (on the application of South Gloucestershire Local Education Authority) v South Gloucestershire Schools Appeal Panel* [2001] EWHC 732 (Admin)] in which an appeal panel had considered the LEA's admission policy for infant class size admissions to be effectively unlawful on the grounds that its criteria for sibling admission lacked any sort of clarity. The actual judgement may though also be put down to its peculiar facts and the sympathy the court showed to a panel which had been faced with an education officer who did not know his own policy and an LEA which hinted it would sack panel members who produced decisions it did not like.

6.5.9   Nonetheless, in his judgment Stanley Burnton J felt that Human Rights Act issues were at play. Thus he indicated that an appeal panel hearing an infant class size appeal could consider the lawfulness of an admissions policy and consider if it infringed the Human Rights Act.

> 'That is not to say that every panel hearing must become a state trial. A panel will normally be entitled to assume that a school's admission policy is lawful and does not infringe the European Convention on Human Rights. If an allegation of infringement of a human right is raised, such as discrimination on the grounds of residence, it will usually be possible to deal with it briefly. If the LEA provides a reasonable explanation and justification for its policy, in most cases that will suffice. If there is a real issue as to the lawfulness of a school's admission policy, the better course, if practicable, is for the panel to defer its decision pending judicial review proceedings.'

Whether the latter point is practicable is possibly debatable and indeed the Court of Appeal in the *Hounslow* case [see 6.5.11*ff* below] disagreed with the judge's suggestion. Nonetheless, the decision might suggest that in any admission appeal, even one involving infant class sizes, if a parent challenges the lawfulness of an admission policy on human rights grounds and even if that is based on the application of the Human Rights Act to their child's individual circumstances, it is open to the appeal panel to consider and determine that point.

6.5.10 More worrying perhaps for LEAs, although this point in the judgment does not appear to have been widely reported, was the judge's *obiter* comments on admission policies which discriminate between siblings and others on the grounds of residence. It does not seem too fanciful to read for 'residence' 'catchment areas', in which case there may be problems for any residential or geographical demarcation. 'I initially felt that discrimination on the basis of residence was not within the scope of Article 14 [*prohibition on discrimination*] of the [Convention], which must be viewed with Article 2 of the First Protocol, which ensures that citizens have a right to education. On reflection, I have concluded that such discrimination is within the scope of Article 14' [at paragraph 54].

6.5.11 In the most recent and authoritative case on these appeals, *R v School Admissions Appeals Panel for Hounslow LBC ex parte Hounslow LBC* [[2002] EWCA Civ 900], the Court of Appeal has provided some clarification and has indicated that the merits of a parents' case are not entirely irrelevant. Although the merits should not be considered by an appeal panel itself, the appeal panel should check to ensure that the admissions authority when refusing admission had taken account of the parents' circumstances and consider whether the authority's decision was unreasonable in light of those circumstances. 'In my view, the fact that the LEA does not have to *comply* with the parental preference does not mean that they do not have to take it [and, it is submitted, the reason for it] into account' [May LJ at paragraph 6]. 'The "circumstances of the case" must, in my view, include the child's particular circumstances including…any preference expressed by the parents' [at paragraph 51] and that therefore the parents had been misinformed by the LEA when it had told them that they could not rely on their individual circumstances. The key question for the panel was therefore whether it was perverse in the light of the admission arrangements to refuse to admit this *particular* child. For example, if an LEA knew that particular circumstances meant that a child could go *only* to the school for which he had been refused admission for health reasons but did not consider those circumstances to see whether the child could be admitted under one of the exceptions to the infant class size duty, it could be held to be acting unreasonably.

6. SCHOOL ORGANISATION

6.5.12 The Court of Appeal also considered the human rights aspects and considered that by its nature an admission policy will discriminate in order to allocate places. The perceived unfairness would be greater in infant class size appeals because of the statutory limit on the parent's preferences. No one suggested, however, that a limit of this kind was other than desirable and so the Court effectively accepted the compatibility of the specific restrictions with the Human Rights Act. Although, therefore, in any type of appeal there would be discrimination, the Court considered that there would be no breach of the Human Rights Act and Article 14 so long as the discrimination in the policy was based on reasonable objective justification and that decisions made under that admissions policy were objectively fair and made by a process which is equally fair [see paragraph 62].

6.5.13 Despite the *Hounslow* clarification, there will still be a few occasions where the panel itself will need to get to grips with parents' circumstances. What, however, if those circumstances raise human rights issues other than the discrimination point or, indeed, other Convention Rights taken together with the inherent discrimination of the policy? For example, the child may have an older sibling at the school, the parents' religious convictions might strengthen the case for their child to be admitted to that school or the child may have been bullied elsewhere and sending him or her to another school could lead to him or her suffering degrading treatment. Can these factors simply be ignored by the panel? Probably not. Appeal panels are public authorities within the Human Rights Act and are under the same duties as any other to ensure that a person's Convention Rights are not infringed. If, by failing to take account of particular circumstances, a panel felt that either the admissions authority or the panel itself would be acting in a way which was incompatible with those rights, it would be, *prima facie*, acting unlawfully. The only defence would be that it was prevented from doing anything else because of the primary legislation, i.e. the SSFA 98. But that may be risky as it could be argued that an admission authority which made a decision which ignored a person's Convention Rights would not be acting as a reasonable admission authority would act and, so, the Human Rights Act point would be relevant to the issue of the reasonableness of the decision. This is pretty circular and to date no answer has been offered by the courts as to whether appeal panels can consider human rights facts, even if they cannot consider personal circumstances. In the rare event that a parent did wish to raise a factor that invoked a potential Convention Right, an appeal panel would probably be wise not to dismiss it out of hand, at least until the Court of Appeal says they can!

6.
SCHOOL
ORGANISATION

7. School Attendance

7.1 Introduction

7.1.1 Securing that children attend schools is a difficult but important task for LEAs which relies on both informal encouragement and formal enforcement. In the past, possibly too much emphasis has been placed on the attempt to persuade, with the result that the Government clearly sees a greater emphasis on enforcement and punishment as a vital weapon to reduce truancy [see, for example, *Failure of truancy crackdowns results in tougher policies*, *The Independent*, 10 October 2002].

7.1.2 Where, however, securing compulsory attendance is concerned and the possibility of prosecuting parents arises, it is possible that the Human Rights Act will have an impact.

7.1.3 This section will therefore consider the impact, if any, of the Human Rights Act on school attendance orders, non-attendance prosecutions, 'truancy sweeps' under the Crime and Disorder Act 1998 and the related subject of school transport provision.

7.2 School attendance orders and non-attendance prosecutions

7.2.1 Under the EA 1996, LEAs have responsibility to take action where it becomes apparent to them that children are not receiving a proper education; in effect, they have the obligation to ensure that parents are meeting their duties under s 7 of the EA 1996 to secure that children of compulsory school age are receiving suitable education by regular attendance at school or otherwise. If a child is not in school and is not receiving education suitable to his or her age, ability and aptitude and to any SEN he or she may have, the LEA is required to serve a notice on the parent or parents requiring them to satisfy the LEA that the child is receiving such education [s 437(1) EA 1996]. If the parent fails to satisfy the LEA and it is expedient that the child should attend school, the LEA must serve a school attendance order on the parent compelling the parent to register the child at the school named in the order [s 437(2) EA 1996]. The detailed procedure leading to the issue of a school attendance order is set out in the EA 1996 [ss 439 to 442]. Once an order is issued, however, if a parent fails to secure that their child attends school in accordance with the order, they are guilty of an offence [s 443 EA 1996] unless they can show to a court that they are causing their child to receive suitable education otherwise than at school.

7.2.2   Where a child has been registered at school, the non-attendance provisions of the EA 1996 apply. Thus, where a child of compulsory school age is a registered pupil at a school and fails to attend regularly his or her parent(s) are guilty of an offence [s 444(1) EA 1996]. Subject to the statutory defences outlined below, this has been treated as an offence of strict liability [*Bath and North East Somerset v Warman* [1999] ELR 81 and *Jarman v Mid-Glamorgan Education Authority* [1985] LS Gaz R 1249].

7.2.3   In addition, the Criminal Justice and Court Services Act 2000 introduced a more serious offence under s 444(1A) where a child fails to attend regularly and the parent knows that he or she is failing to attend and, without reasonable justification, fails to cause him or her to do so. A person guilty of an offence under s 444(1A) is liable on summary conviction to a fine not exceeding level 4 on the standard scale, or to imprisonment for a term not exceeding three months, or both. In contrast, a person guilty under s 444 (1) can be liable only to a fine not exceeding level 3 on the standard scale [s 444(8) and (8A) EA 1996].

7.2.4   It has been held that there can be a failure to attend regularly where a child frequently arrives after the attendance register has been closed [*Hinchley v Rankin* [1961] 1 All ER 692] and also where a child is sent to school dressed in such a way that the parent knows the head teacher will refuse admission for failure to comply with school rules [*Spiers v Warrington Corporation* [1954] 1 QB 61]. Whether the latter is still valid is a matter of debate and will be considered below [see Chapter 8].

7.2.5   Defences are available to parents: if the child is absent with leave; at any time when the child was prevented from attending by reason of sickness or any unavoidable cause; or on any day exclusively set apart for religious observance by the religious body to which his or her parent belongs [s 444(3)]. In addition the child shall not be taken to have failed to attend regularly at the school if the parent proves that the school at which the child is a registered pupil is not within walking distance of the child's home, and that no suitable arrangements have been made by the local education authority for any of the following: (i) transport to and from the school; (ii) boarding accommodation at or near the school; or (iii) enabling the child to become a registered pupil at a school nearer to home [s 444(4) EA 1996]. Special provisions are made to deal with children of 'traveller' parents [s 444(6) EA 1996].

7.2.6   'Unavoidable cause' has, however, been held to relate only to the child; circumstances affecting the parent have not been considered to provide a valid defence [*Jenkins v Howells* [1949] 2 KB 218]. In *R v Havering London Borough Council, ex p K* [(1997) 96 LGR 325], it was held that 'unavoidable cause' was capable of including want of transport although on the facts the lack of transport did not satisfy the threshold. Non-attendance on days of religious observance could clearly have implications with regard to Articles 9 and 14 and it is important that there be no discrimination between different religions. Under UK law, Ascension Day is apparently a day exclusively set apart by the Church of England [*Marshall v Graham, Bell v Graham* [1970] 2 KB 112, 76 LJKB 690] but the courts have not determined what other religious days count as days of observance. If these issues arise in the future it is likely that the courts will look to the Convention and Strasbourg jurisprudence for assistance. There should be no difficulty over recognised religions, but problems may occur in respect of the less well-recognised religions and with other faiths or beliefs. If humanists sets aside a day for humanist contemplation, could a parent keep their child at home? The Commission was prepared to accept that druidism was a religion [*Chappel v United Kingdom* Application No 12587/86, (1987) 53 DR 241] and that Jehovah's Witnesses formed a known religion [*Kokkinakis v Greece* (1993) Series A No 260-A 17 EHRR 397] so there may be the opportunity for some flexibility. Simple assertions that a particular religion exists are not enough; claiming to be a 'Wicca' is not sufficient without proof of its existence [*X v United Kingdom* (1977) 11 DR 55] and presumably, despite the census returns, the ECtHR would not recognise Jedi as a religion either, or Jedi Knights as its adherents.

7.2.7   Whatever is a religion, however, Article 9 has not established a right of exemption from disciplinary rules which are, in effect, not discriminatory. In *Valsamis v Greece* [[1998] ELR 430], parents who were Jehovah's Witnesses asked that their daughter be excused from school RE lessons and any event contrary to their religious beliefs, including national celebrations. The child refused to take part in a national day parade and was suspended as a result. The ECtHR held there had been no breach of the right to education, but did not really consider the question of the parent's rights under Article 9. What *Valsamis* suggests though, is that parents should, as English law provides, be permitted to keep their children off school on days of religious observance. But their religion does not give them permission to keep their children at home on days where a school is doing something which is against that religion.

7.2.8   Issues relating to transport are considered further below at 7.5.

7.2.9   The main concerns which have been expressed about these provisions in the context of the Human Rights Act principally relate to: the compatibility of the prosecution of these offences as, effectively, offences of strict liability; the powers available to LEAs to inspect and adjudge whether a parent is providing suitable education; and the introduction of 'truancy sweeps'.

7.2.10   The legality of a prosecution under s 444 has been considered in respect of similar provisions in Scottish legislation but, albeit only in a decision of a Sheriff, that decision could have had worrying implications for enforcement proceedings south of the border, especially if the Secretary of State wants to establish a 'get tough' policy against parents of truants.

7.2.11   Section 35 of the Education (Scotland) Act 1980 provides that where a child of school age 'fails without reasonable excuse to attend regularly' at school, the parent shall be guilty of an offence. A 'reasonable excuse' is deemed to exist in the event of certain circumstances relating to the child's journey to school, the child's sickness or in 'other circumstances' which in the opinion of the education authority or court may afford a reasonable excuse [s 42 Education (Scotland) Act 1980]. As in England and Wales, the reasonable excuse must relate to the child, not the parent [*Kiely v Lunn* 1983 SLT 207 and *Macintyre v Annan* 1991 SCCR 465]. The legislation differs only in the way that the English legislation refers to reasonable justification and unavoidable cause, whereas the two concepts in Scotland are referred to as reasonable excuse and 'other circumstances... which afford a reasonable excuse'. Arguably, the Scottish version could be read as providing a wider range of circumstances which could found a defence, whereas in England only an 'unavoidable cause' will do. That may cause even more problems if the Scottish Sheriff's decision in *O'Hagan v Rea* [2001 SLT (Sh Ct) 30] is to be followed.

7.2.12   In *O'Hagan* a parent was prosecuted for failing to secure the attendance of her child. She argued that the provisions of the 1980 Act were incompatible with Article 6 and the Sheriff agreed. 'Those liable to be found guilty if prosecuted include many who have done nothing wrong and who are, for all practical purposes, unable to affect the factual situation which gives rise to strict liability. They include some parents who have done their best to force their child to attend school and remain there until the end of the school day, but whose efforts have been in vain'. The Sheriff thus reflected the concern that the legislation enables the prosecution of parents who are physically unable to force their children to school (typically the five foot nothing single mother with the six foot tall 15 year old), parents who may have no care and control of the child (although hopefully LEAs would exercise their discretion sensibly and not prosecute separated parents) and parents who get their children to school in the morning but then discover that they truant for the afternoon. Instinctively, the Sheriff felt that such parents should not be subject to criminal sanctions. He therefore concluded that 'section 35 [of the 1980 Act] does not provide the accused with any defence arising out of his practical innocence, whether based on force majeure, reasonable diligence or the like.'

7.2.13 Noting in particular that the court could refer the child to a principal reporter of the children's panel (effectively the equivalent of an education supervision order in England and Wales), the Sheriff held that 'the conviction of the parent cannot be seen as being indispensable to the aims of the legislation [to secure attendance] and so strict liability is more difficult to justify. It seems to me that the imposition of strict liability on the parent of a truanting child can properly be described as arbitrary, unfair and, in any event, more onerous than is necessary to compel parents to do their best to secure the regular attendance of her children at school.' *Prima facie* therefore he held the legislation to be incompatible with the Human Rights Act. However, he then went onto consider how it could be rendered compatible and concluded that this could be a fairly simple task provided that a wide meaning was given to the words 'reasonable excuse' so that it could include circumstances relating to the parents as well as the child.

7. SCHOOL ATTENDANCE

7.2.14 *O'Hagan* is admittedly a Scottish case and is not binding on the English courts. In the one English case on the point, *Barnfather v Islington LBC and the Secretary of State for Education and Skills* [[2003] EWHC 418 (Admin)], the High Court held that s 444(1) and (1A) were compatible with the Human Rights Act. S 444(1A) caused the court few problems as the offence under that sub-section requires the prosecution to prove that the parent knew the child was failing to attend. S 444(1) on the other hand requires no knowledge on the part of the parent and it did give the court some difficulties. Nonetheless, and although Elias J questioned the fact that s 444(1) should effectively allow the prosecution of the innocent, the court held that Article 6 did not entitle the courts to question the justification for strict liability offences. Hence, the prosecutions were human rights compatible. Although the court referred to the O'Hagan decision, it did not give any reasons why it felt that that decision was incorrect, which does, therefore, still leave a question over the legality of non-attendance prosecutions which may require answering in a higher court. It would therefore seem that prosecutions for non-attendance are still legally possible (indeed, desirable – for a failure to initiate action against a defaulting parent could give the child the potential to bring an action under Article 2 of the First Protocol if he or she was denied an education as a result [see

7.2.15*ff* below]). LEAs should perhaps be cautious, however, in bringing prosecutions where a parent 'does not have the child living with him and who is both ignorant and effectively powerless in relation to the child's truancy' or in the case of a 'single mother who is incapable of persuading or forcing a school-phobic 15 year old to attend and remain at school' [*O'Hagan v Rea* at paragraph 7].

7.2.15 An interesting issue is the responsibility of the LEA to take action to protect the child. This should not apply where the child is complicit in the truancy but what if the child has the misfortune to have a parent who cannot be bothered to make him or her go to school or, even worse, encourages the truancy so that the child can help him or her at work or at home? Indeed, this latter more serious default was recognised as such by the creation of the new s 444(1A) offence.

7. SCHOOL ATTENDANCE

7.2.16 For some time there has been concern that LEAs have not been enforcing non-attendance as stringently as they might; does the Human Rights Act impose greater obligations on them to do so? Any claim would be framed under Article 2 of the First Protocol in the sense that the LEA's failure had denied the child access to education. No claim has, it is thought, yet been made and the probability is that the courts would be loath to interfere in an authority's decision whether to prosecute or not. In the public law context, the courts have left significant discretion to, for example, the Attorney General and Director of Public Prosecutions. It is not inconceivable, however, that, in an extreme case, if an LEA's attention had been drawn to a child who they knew was not receiving suitable education, and they failed to act so the child was never admitted into a school or received any education, that child could subsequently invoke Article 2 of the First Protocol.

7.2.17 Related to this is, in fact, the power of an LEA to obtain information about the failure of a parent to secure their child's attendance and the means by which they can satisfy themselves that whatever provision is being made is suitable. Where it becomes apparent to an LEA that a child of compulsory school age in its area is not receiving suitable education, either by regular attendance or otherwise, the LEA is under a duty to serve a notice in writing on the parent requiring him or her to satisfy the LEA that within a specified period the child is receiving suitable education [s 437(1) EA 1996]. 'Suitable education' means 'efficient full-time education suitable to his age, ability and aptitude and to any SEN he may have' [s 437(8) EA 1996 and see *R v Gwent County Council, ex p Perry* (1985) 129 Sol Jo 737, in which the Court of Appeal considered the procedures followed by the LEA to satisfy themselves as to whether a child, taught by his parents at home, was receiving full-time education suitable to his age, ability and aptitude;

Bevan v Shears (1911) (efficiency of education provided); *R v Walton Justices, ex p Dutton* (1911) 75 JP 558 (evidence of the state of child's education); *R v West Riding of Yorkshire Justices, ex p Broadbent* [1910] 2 KB 192 (efficiency of alternative education); *Osborne v Martin* (1927) 91 JP 197 (withdrawal from school for piano lessons); and *Baker v Earl* (1960) *The Times*, 6 February (where the parent occupied, but did not educate, his children at home)].

7.2.18 Clearly if a parent can show that their child is attending school they should be able to satisfy the LEA. But what if they refuse to respond? Could they argue that their children's education is a private matter and the request infringes Article 8 – respect for private and family life? Alternatively, what if the parents say that they are making provision at home, but they refuse to provide details or allow the LEA into their home to check? Can they too argue that they are able to do so because of Article 8?

7.2.19 In the former case, the decision of parents as to their children's education is probably part of, or an adjunct to, their family life. In principle, then, any questioning by an LEA as to education provided is *prima facie* an interference with their private or family life. It is unlikely, however, to be unlawful under Article 8. First, Article 8 is a right to have private and family life respected; an LEA's questioning, if based on valid concerns, is not necessarily going to be disrespectful. Clearly, as in all actions which may fall within the Human Rights Act, an authority must respect views and opinions where appropriate, but showing respect does not equate to accepting and being bound by them. Second, and perhaps more importantly, even if there is interference, Article 8 is a qualified right. It could, the author believes, be shown that the interference was in accordance with the law (i.e. such action is clearly required by s 437 EA 1996); and is necessary (where the LEA has reasonable and genuine concerns that a child is not receiving education or attending school) in a democratic society for, certainly, the protection of the rights and freedoms of others (i.e. the child) and, possibly, for the protection of health or morals or, if the evidence that many truants commit crime is correct, the prevention of disorder or crime.

7.2.20 With regard to the issue of how an LEA can satisfy itself as to the provision, the Human Rights Act may create a few problems, but may not actually affect the ability of the LEA to proceed towards a school attendance order. The logical view must be that in order to be satisfied, the LEA should be able to see the provision being made. Where children are being educated at home, that will mean entering the home. Can the parents use Article 8 to deny them that access? Probably, yes. That would most probably be seen as a *prima facie* interference with the parents' family life. The LEA could not force their way in as they have no statutory right of entry, so that sort of interference would not be 'in accordance with the law' and hence the qualifications to Article 8 could not be applied. Article 8 may therefore well prevent an LEA requiring a parent to show it what provision was being made.

7.2.21 This is not, however, the same as saying that this could, in effect, permit an obstructive parent to prevent an LEA ever proceeding to issue a school attendance order. The reason is that s 437 places the onus on the parent to satisfy the LEA that the provision is suitable. If the parent does not tell the LEA what he or she is doing or refuses to allow the LEA to see, it is hard to see that the LEA can ever be satisfied. Indeed, it might be acting improperly if it did say it was satisfied without considering the provision. Thus, if the parent cannot satisfy the LEA, the LEA is obliged to proceed to the next stage and serve notice on the parent of its intent to serve a school attendance order [s 438 EA 1996]. Article 8 rights may therefore merely have academic interest in this process.

7.2.22 A further issue about attendance enforcement is raised by the SEN case of *CB v Merton LBC* [and see 10.1.12 below]. In that case parents had argued that the decision of the SENT to name a residential school in their child's statement of SEN was an infringement of their Article 8 rights. The court held that the naming of a school did not amount to an 'interference' with that right and so upheld the SENT's decision. Unfortunately, though, the rationale for that decision does raise potential problems in the attendance context. This is because the court felt able to say that the naming of a school merely facilitated the child's attendance and did not therefore amount to an interference with their family life. The LEA was obliged to name the school in the statement and if it had to issue a school attendance order the named school would also have to be named in the SAO [s 441(2) EA 1996]. But it would be for the LEA (as enforcer of school attendance not as the body responsible for SEN) to decide whether an SAO should be served and whether it would be appropriate to commence enforcement proceedings in the magistrates court. The judge accepted that Article 8 might then be engaged at that point under the EA 1996; but it would not be the act of naming the school that would expose the parent to prosecution. Rather, it would be the parent's failure to ensure that the child was receiving a suitable education that would expose the parent to the risk of prosecution. In the meantime between the school being named and the enforcement action, the parent 'is at liberty to make whatever other arrangements for the [child's] education as she feels appropriate'.

7.2.23 What this does mean for attendance enforcement is perhaps not too clear. It is probably authority to suggest that forcing a child to attend a residential school by threatening to prosecute a parent if they fail to attend is an interference with the right to have a private and family life respected. That said, it is a qualified right and if the action is taken in accordance with the law (and it should be – the school should have been named in a statement of SEN in accordance with the provisions of Part IV of the EA 1996, with the parents having the right to appeal; and the enforcement action would be taken under s 443 and the preceding sections of the EA 1996), it should fall within the qualifications to Article 8. It will then be a question of whether the interference is necessary in a democratic society in the interest of the protection of the rights and freedoms of others, the protection of health or morals, etc., and proportionate. Again, so long as the school has been named in accordance with the relevant legislation, the SEN Code of Practice and was an educationally sound decision, it is unlikely that the interference will amount to a breach of Article 8.

7.2.24 Would there be any difference if the SAO was to name a non-residential school, i.e. a mainstream day school or a special day school? Probably not. One difference, though, might be whether there was actually any interference with Article 8 simply by naming such a school. Unlike with residential provision, family life could be enjoyed outside school hours; it would only be during school hours where there was any compulsion which would separate the family. Is this in fact interference with 'private and family life'? Possibly is perhaps the best answer which can be currently given. It is not inconceivable that the courts will interpret education to be a significant part of a person's development which is recognised as being an important part of their private life [see, for example, *Niemietz v FRG* (1992) Series A No 251-B (1993) 16 EHRR 97]. Whether there is interference or not, however, it is nonetheless probable that if the LEA have acted in accordance with the statutory process and can show that requiring a child to attend the named school is in his or her educational interests, no court would hold the LEA in breach of Article 8.

7.3   Religious observance

7.3.1 Before leaving the subject of non-attendance, one further area where the Human Rights Act may have an impact is where it is claimed that a child was unable to attend on a day set aside for religious observance. Previous UK cases have given 'religious' in this context a domestic meaning. It is probable that, in future, courts would be more inclined to give it the meaning found in the Convention and given by the ECtHR [see 5.3.4*ff* above].

7.4 Truancy sweeps

7.4.1 Next in this section we need to look at the recent introduction of truancy sweeps under the Crime and Disorder Act 1998. If a police officer has reasonable cause to believe that a child found by him or her in a public place within an area specified by a superintendent is of compulsory school age and is absent from school without lawful authority, the officer may remove him or her to premises designated by the LEA or to the school from which he or she is absent [s 16(3) Crime and Disorder Act 1998].

7.4.2 It is unlikely that most of the Convention Rights will come into play. An ingenious child might argue that the officer would be interfering with his or her freedom of association (Article 11) or possible that he or she was being detained contrary to his or her right to liberty (Article 5). With the former, Article 11 is a qualified right, the action would be prescribed by law; there is clearly a strong argument that it is necessary in a democratic society in the interests of the rights and freedoms of others, public safety, the prevention of disorder or crime or for the protection of health or morals, quite possibly the child's; and the action should be proportionate.

7.4.3 The latter, Article 5 point, may be more problematic. Such deprivation of liberty as there is could potentially be justified as the 'lawful arrest or detention of a person...in order to secure the fulfilment of any obligation prescribed by law' or 'the detention of a minor by lawful order for the purpose of educational supervision or his lawful detention for the purpose of bringing him before the competent legal authority'. The problem with the former is that there is no obligation on the child, i.e. the person being detained, the obligation rests on the parents. Whether 'obligations' could be interpreted as including obligations owed by third parties is probably unlikely so the latter justification is the one which should avail the police and LEAs, although they must ensure that wherever the child is taken, he or she will receive some form of educational supervision.

7.4.4 As school attendance is closely associated with enforcement action where courts are particularly keen to ensure no infringement of human rights, this may be an area which features in litigation in the future. Nonetheless, if both LEAs and courts adopt a sensible attitude, especially towards the prosecution of 'fault free' parents, there should not be a substantial impact on the work of education welfare officers.

7.
SCHOOL
ATTENDANCE

7.5 School transport

7.5.1 Finally, in this chapter it is necessary to look at the provision of school transport in the context of the Human Rights Act. Given the disputes over transport under UK law [see, for example, *George v Devon County Council* [1988] 3 All ER 1002 through to *R v Gwent County Council ex p Harris* [1995] ELR 27] it is surprising that no Human Rights Act case has yet appeared.

7.5.2 Nonetheless, the topic has raised press interest [see, for example, *'Sikh girl denied free school bus because of her religion'*, *The Independent*, 10 September 2002] and it is therefore conceivable that human rights issues may arise in the future. If so, how?

7.5.3 An LEA is under a duty to make arrangements for the provision of transport and otherwise as it considers necessary for the purpose of facilitating the attendance of persons receiving education [s 509 EA 1996]. The duty is therefore ancillary to the LEA's responsibilities to secure that children attend schools. In considering whether it is required to make such arrangements in respect of a particular person, the LEA must have regard, amongst other things, to a) the age of the person and the nature of the route or alternative routes which they could reasonably be expected to take and b) any wish of the parent for the child to be provided with education at a school or institution in which the religious education provided is that of the religion or denomination to which the parent adheres [s 509(4) EA 1996].

7. SCHOOL ATTENDANCE

7.5.4 This later provision therefore to a certain extent foreshadowed the Human Rights Act and the freedom of religion in Article 9 and the respect for parents' convictions in Article 2 of the First Protocol, though probably not deliberately. It should, however, mean that, so long as LEAs do have regard to parents' wishes, there should not be too many human rights breaches. The problem, as appears from the case reported by *The Independent*, would be where the parent may have religious convictions for believing their child should attend a particular denominational school, but they do not adhere to the school's religion or denomination. In the case of the Sikh family, they wished their daughter to attend a Roman Catholic school instead of the local community school because there was no Sikh school nearby and they wanted 'the better, stricter education they believed faith schools offered'. Under s 509, the LEA offered free transport to Catholic families, but not to families who were not of the Catholic faith.

7.5.5   There seems no doubt that in many cases, transport provision is inextricably linked to the parents' preference for a school. Whilst it may not be the case that the lack of transport would deny a child education (assuming there are places at closer schools) under the first limb of Article 2 of the First Protocol, in making transport provision, LEAs should have regard to parents' religious (and, if relevant, philosophical) convictions. This would, it is suggested, mean that limiting their regard to only those families of the same faith as the school which they wish their children to attend would no longer be enough. They must, via the second limb of Article 2 of the First Protocol, also have regard to all other religious and philosophical convictions. By analogy with the *Newham* case [*R (on the application of K) v Newham LBC* [[2002] EWHC 405 (Admin)] and see 6.3.3 above], in making arrangements for transport, LEAs should enable parents to express their convictions and take them into account. This is not, of course, determinative – the LEA only needs to respect these convictions – but is something LEAs should consider including within their transport policies as well as their admissions policies. That should then avoid any allegation of discrimination between different faiths and religions. It is suggested though that parental preferences for their children to be transported by taxi or only on buses with seatbelts [see, *R v Gwent County Council ex p Harris* [1995] ELR 27] would not be convictions sufficient for these purposes.

SCHOOL
ATTENDANCE

7.5.6   Other Convention Rights are unlikely to come into play with transport. Potentially LEAs would need to ensure that children are not transported in cattle trucks or by routes of unreasonable length and circuity (a possible Article 3 – inhuman or degrading treatment matter) but that is already prohibited under United Kingdom [see the stress free transport case *R v Hereford and Worcester County Council ex p P* [1992] 2 FCR 732]. But even then, the level of 'poor' treatment would have to be particularly severe to engage Article 3, albeit the age and needs of the children being carried would be factors which could lower the threshold of severity.

8. School Rules, Discipline and Exclusions

8.1 Introduction

8.1.1 To the layman, school discipline and exclusions might initially appear to be an area where the Human Rights Act would have a significant impact. After all, the punishing of a child and, more particularly, their exclusion from school, can have a dramatic effect on their education. Surely, then, it must be an area where the actions of schools will receive greater scrutiny?

8.1.2 Logic, however, does not appear to have triumphed here over legal interpretation. Although the courts have given broad hints that at some future date they may take a more interventionist approach [see the comments of Schliemann LJ in *S, T, P v Brent LBC and Others* [2002] EWCA Civ 693 at para 30], the Human Rights Act has, perhaps surprisingly, had little impact or operation.

8.1.3 This, as we will see, is principally due to the case of *Simpson v United Kingdom* [64 DR 188 (1989) and see 8.7.20*ff* below] but nonetheless, the Human Rights Act could still be cited in respect of a number of actions relating to discipline in schools and pupil referral units.

8.2 School discipline

8.2.1 Schools have rules. Under national law, provided that they are 'reasonable' and relevant, they are *prima facie* lawful. Problems may come with the enforcement of some of them, for example, in respect of school uniform, but by and large schools adopt and enforce them without too much difficulty and with, in relative terms, only the occasional objection.

Corporal Punishment

8.2.2 Corporal punishment has been abolished now in all schools as a result of the ECtHR decisions in *Campbell and Cosans v United Kingdom* [(1982) 4 EHRR 293] and *Costello-Roberts v United Kingdom* [(1993) Series A No 247-C, 19 EHRR 112], which established that a parent's objection to corporal punishment was a philosophical conviction under Article 2 of the First Protocol which had to be respected. The decisions led to the UK Government, in effect, prohibiting such punishment through ss 47 to 48 of the Education (No 2) Act 1986 and now s 548 EA 1996 as amended.

8.2.3   Will religious or philosophical convictions prevent other forms of discipline being administered? It is submitted that this is unlikely. In *Williamson v Secretary of State for Education and Employment* [[2001] EWHC Admin 960 (Admin) and [2002] EWCA Civ 1820], Elias J, who was upheld by the Court of Appeal, made clear that the courts would protect the right to object to corporal punishment on the basis that the law had always shown a respect for an individual's physical integrity (although not expressly stated, the judge was perhaps recognising that the children's Article 8 rights had to be balanced) and stronger reason was required to justify the right to inflict physical injury.

8.2.4   That being the case, a parent's belief that their child should not be subject to any form of discipline or should only be subject to punishment of which they approve is unlikely to be treated as a 'conviction'. Indeed, *Williamson* perhaps shows, albeit in the extreme case of parents who felt it was part of their religious beliefs that their children should receive corporal punishment, that so long as schools act reasonably, the courts will not permit parents to impose their views, whether pro-discipline or anti-discipline, on head teachers.

8.2.5   Consequently, provided other forms of punishment are adopted which do not inflict physical injury and do not constitute inhuman or degrading treatment, schools should continue to feel confident in their ability to administer them.

8.3   Detention

8.3.1   Detention is perhaps one which might raise some concern, especially in light of Article 5 – the right to liberty and security. Does detaining a child contravene their right to liberty? In the first place, Article 5 itself states that the right to liberty is not infringed by 'the detention of a minor by lawful order for the purpose of educational supervision' [Article 5(1)(d)]. Whether this really envisages school detention as opposed to the type of education provided at the time the Convention was drafted, i.e. educational provision akin to secure educational units or reform schools, is debatable. But, going back to the point about the Convention protecting fundamental rights, if it is envisaged that the right to liberty would not be infringed by detaining children in secure units for educational purposes, it is unlikely that detaining them at lunchtime or after school on one off occasions as a consequence of their misbehaviour is likely to fall foul of Article 5 either.

8.3.2 Further, in *Family TV v Austria* [64 DR 176 (1989)], it was held that a punitive detention does not in any event involve any deprivation of liberty falling within Article 5 so long as no greater restrictions are imposed than are a normal incident of bringing up children.

8.3.3 Consequently, it is suggested that detention in itself will not infringe Article 5. Schools must, nonetheless, continue to comply with domestic law and ensure that any detention imposed meets the conditions set out in s 550B EA 1996, otherwise the safeguards set out above may well fall away.

8.3.4 Other punishments short of detention are also likely to be permissible. The test will be the extent of the humiliation and whether, if that is high, the punishment will amount to degrading treatment under Article 3. Lines, making a child stand in the naughty corner or going to see the head teacher for a dressing down are unlikely to amount to this. It has been suggested that sending a child out to run round a playing field in the snow and wind or parading them in front of the whole school could be sufficiently humiliating [see *Local Authorities and the Human Rights Act 1998,* Supperstone, Goudie and Coppel at page 62], but even that level of treatment is arguably not above the threshold of mistreatment envisaged in Article 3 and held unlawful by the ECtHR. Nonetheless, if the threat of action under the Human Rights Act reins in the sadistic sports master, that may be no bad thing.

8.4 Confiscation

8.4.1 Another form of punishment is confiscation of items which the school prohibits being brought into class. Mobile phones and Pokémon cards seem to be the most contentious items currently on the list of prohibited goods. Does this action infringe a child's human rights? From personal experience, the author can recount two complaints from parents that confiscation had infringed their child's human rights: the first concerned a knife, the second a boa constrictor. The first was serious and, as will be seen, arguments that this action did not infringe anyone's human rights were made to justify the action and not challenged. In the second, the main complaint was that the school's confiscation of the snake infringed its own rules. The father's grievance was that the school rules said 'No pets are allowed into school' but the snake was not a pet, rather part of his wife's somewhat exotic stage act. But the author probably digresses.

8.4.2 The issue is whether an act of confiscation infringes the Convention Right protecting a person's property under Article 1 of the First

Protocol. Certainly the seizing of any goods by a teacher is likely to amount to an infringement of the child's or parent's peaceful enjoyment of their possessions. However, if this matter ever came to court, most confiscations could be justified by reference to the qualifications to Article 1 of the First Protocol, i.e. that no person may be deprived of their possession except in the public interest and subject to the conditions provided for by law. There is nothing in UK law to suggest that confiscation is unlawful *per se* (although it is suggested that a school should make it clear in its policies and prospectus that it may use this sanction) and clearly in many cases it will be justified in the public interest, certainly as far as weapons, dangerous items and drugs are concerned (although again schools need to be careful as to when they should take this action or involve the police). This may make it more difficult to confiscate the mobile phone or the cards, but even here it is arguable that so long as the school has objective justification for believing that their possession in school would be detrimental to the public interest, or more specifically the interests of other pupils and staff in the school, they could defend their actions. With phones and Pokémon cards, apart from the nuisance which may be caused, the fact that they can lead to theft and fights might also be a valid reason.

8.5   School uniform

8.5.1   The issue of school uniform has caused considerable problems for schools under United Kingdom law. So, the introduction of the Human Rights Act, and especially the freedom of expression under Article 10, may lead to a school uniform rule being challenged at some point in the future.

8.5.2   Under domestic law, the position can best be summarised as confused. Advice issued by the DfEE in 1987 [DfE Circular 7/87 *Education (No 2) Act 1986: Further Guidance*] advised that governing bodies could decide whether school uniform should be worn and, if so, what, provided they had regard to the LEA's policy on uniform grants and other relevant circumstances at their school. In principle, if a parent refuses to send their child to school in the correct uniform, the school could refuse to admit and the parent would be prosecuted for failing to secure the attendance of their child [see *Spiers v Warrington Corporation* [1954] 1 QB 61]. However, that position must have been weakened a) by the age of the case, b) by the fact that it pre-dated the current rules on exclusion and c) because it concerned a girl who wanted to wear trousers at a time when a court felt it permissible to require girls to wear skirts. Sadly, the latter point has not been clarified in the courts; a recent challenge to such a policy was settled out of court [*'Once more unto the breeches'*, *TES*, 4 June 1999]. It is not hard to imagine that a ban on girls wearing trousers would already infringe the Sex Discrimination Act 1975, before we need consider the Human Rights Act. Similarly, schools need to ensure that their policies do not discriminate against the dress of particular ethnic or racial groups and so infringe the Race Relations Act 1976.

8.5.3   Where the Human Rights Act may add to a school's difficulties is if a pupil asserts that they wish to wear a particular item of clothing, sport a particular tattoo or embroider 'Stuff the School' or worse on the back of their school blazer. Would an attempt to punish the pupil be an infringement of their freedom of expression under Article 10? In principle, the statement being made is an expression on the part of the pupil whether in the type of clothing, word or the message being conveyed. Indeed, there would be no difference between this and the child who stands up in class and tells his teacher that his teaching sucks, or, again, worse. They are all expressions of opinion which Article 10 *prima facie* protects.

8.5.4   However, accepting that pupils can say whatever they want and challenge the authority of school staff would clearly lead to anarchy and a classroom environment not dissimilar to the House of Commons. Some opinions will more evidently be worthy of greater protection. Valid questioning or challenging of a teacher's opinion should be permitted, as should the expression of reasonable political views or criticisms of particular conduct. Whistleblowing in schools is not expressly protected, but where justified, should be under Article 10.

8.5.5   But there will be limits and the qualifications to Article 10 would appear to permit a school to take action where those limits were breached, both in terms of what a pupil says and what a pupil wears or displays. Thus, the freedom, because it carries with it duties and responsibilities, may be subject to such formalities, conditions, restrictions or penalties as are prescribed by law and are necessary in a democratic society in the interests of, amongst others, public safety, the prevention of disorder or crime, the protection of health or morals, or the protection of the rights or reputations of others. Within that mass of qualifications, a school should be able to find a justification for preventing what is unreasonable in terms of uniform and other types of expression but not for what is, in the current society, unduly severe or unrealistic restrictions. Thus, unacceptable political views, whether spoken or apparent, on uniform, racist taunts and BNP badges, clothing which incites drugs use [there is some, apparently] and defamatory or criminally abusive conduct should still be capable of prohibition after the Human Rights Act, but the days of school uniform policies prescribing that 'girls must wear "robust, blue knickers', as once came to the author's attention, are hopefully long gone.

8.5.6 Free speech within schools must therefore, even after the Human Rights Act, continue to have its limits, and uniform policies too, so long as the requirements are reasonable, not unduly expensive for the parents at the school and, if possible, agreed after consultation with parents should continue to be permissible.

8.5.7 One aspect of uniform policy though which causes special problems is the wearing of jewellery, especially in an age where piercing of every conceivable part of one's body is becoming increasing popular. First, schools should always be aware of the particular requirements of certain ethnic and racial groups and prepare their policies accordingly. Second, the wearing of jewellery, as with all other clothing, can be seen as an 'expression' by the wearer which *prima facie* enjoys protection under Article 10. Third, therefore, any ban on jewellery must fall within one of the qualifications set out in 8.5.5 above otherwise it could amount to an unlawful interference.

8.5.8 Here, there may be distinctions to be drawn as to the circumstances when jewellery is worn. For example, during PE and games lessons, a prohibition on jewellery can most probably be justified on health and safety grounds, for the protection of health; either the child's or other pupil's. If the item cannot be removed for those lessons or taped over or other action taken, that could justify a total ban on wearing that item to school. If the item can be easily removed, that justification may disappear and the school would have to rely on one of the other justifications to sustain its policy. Sex discrimination could be an issue (under Article 10, read with Article 14) so that girls should not be treated less favourably than boys and vice versa in the terms of what is permissible and what is not.

8.6 Bullying

8.6.1 One aspect of school life which may have Human Rights Act implications and is probably best considered in this chapter as anywhere else, is the vexed question of bullying.

8.6.2 Bullying has implications, both in terms of what action a school can take against the bully (which has been considered in terms of discipline as set out above and exclusion in appropriate cases as set out below) but also in terms of the action that a school must take to protect the victim.

8.6.3   The reason is simple. Bullying in certain severe cases can amount to inhuman or degrading treatment. The fact that the school itself is not meting out the treatment is neither here nor there, for, as a public authority, it has a positive, pro-active duty to protect those for whom it is responsible from such treatment perpetrated by others.

8.6.4   Already, under the domestic law of negligence, schools have been sued for failing to prevent a pupil being bullied, although no case has yet been successful at trial. In a well reported case involving Richmond upon Thames LBC, settlement was reached before trial on economic grounds and in the two cases which went to trial, the Court of Appeal, in *Bradford-Smart v West Sussex County Council* [[2002] EWCA Civ 07, [2002] ELR 139], rejected the claim on its facts, as did Wright J in the other case, *H v Isle of Wight Council* [[2001] All ER (D) 315 (Feb), QBD].

8.6.5   Nonetheless, now that the Human Rights Act is in force, schools should consider that their duties to deal with bullies, if not necessarily more onerous, may be subject to greater scrutiny. The failure to take action which as a consequence leads to severe cases of bullying may be harder to justify and claims may feature allegations that the victim's rights under Article 3 have been infringed by the school's act, or more probably, omissions.

8.7   Exclusion and exclusion appeals

8.7.1   'Permanent exclusion...has a radical impact on the choice of school, the continuity of schooling and the future prospects of the pupil. The injury capable of being done by it to a child's socialisation and self-esteem is incalculable. It is estimated that about half the male prison population has been the subject of permanent exclusion from school. Equally, schools cannot function as places of learning and social development in an ambience of violence and abuse, whether directed at teachers or at other pupils, or of misconduct or disorder. Pretty well every decision about exclusion is a negotiation between these anxious and competing considerations [per Schiemann LJ *S, T and P v Brent LBC and Others* [2002] EWCA Civ 693].'

8.7.2   How then may the Human Rights Act have an impact on this important and quasi-criminal, quasi-judicial aspect of education?

8.7.3   Exclusion in itself will not infringe a person's right to education. 'The right to education [i.e. Article 2 of the First Protocol] ...is not a right to be educated in a particular school' [*S,T,P* supra, paragraph 9]. So a pupil cannot complain that being excluded from a particular school infringes his or her right; the assumption being that there will be a place elsewhere for them.

8.7.4 This comment follows on from the ECtHR's recognition that such disciplinary sanctions may be necessary. In *Sulak v Turkey* [84-A DR 98 (1996)], a student was expelled from university after he had been caught cheating in an examination for the third time. The Commission held that the right to education did not, in principle, prevent educational institutions having recourse to disciplinary measures, including suspension and expulsion.

8.7.5 In that decision, the Commission did note that the student had the chance to challenge the exclusion at a national level. That is important as it suggest that, although exclusion may be lawful, it must comply with the principles of Article 6 – a right to a fair hearing.

8.7.6 That in turn, though, does call into question whether *Simpson* [for further discussion of this important case see Chapters 6 and 10 and 8.7.25*ff* below] is applicable to exclusions; which may be critical when we come to look at pupil disciplinary committees and independent appeal panels.

8.7.7 The process and rules for excluding pupils are well documented and, although subject to much comment in the press and revised guidance from the DfES, have not altered much in the last few years. The principles are now set out in s 52 of the Education Act 2002 and in the regulations [Education (Pupil Exclusions and Appeals) (Maintained Schools) (England) Regulations 2002, SI 2002/3178] made under that section.

8.7.8 There are two types of exclusion: fixed term for a certain number of specified days (which cannot amount to more than 45 school days in any school year) and permanent, which sees the pupil excluded from the school for good.

8.7.9 Only a head teacher or a person acting as such in the head teacher's absence can exclude a pupil [s 52(1) Education Act 2002]. Whilst the courts have been shy of imposing police standards of scrutiny on teachers responsible for investigating disciplinary incidents and then deciding to exclude a pupil, nonetheless such investigations should be rigorous, fair and based on proper evidence. These principles have been established in domestic cases and it is doubtful that at this point in the exclusion process, the Human Rights Act adds anything, certainly in terms of Article 6.

8.7.10 Convention Rights which may, however, impact on a decision whether or not to exclude may include Article 3 – freedom from torture, inhuman or degrading treatment. This is not so much from the angle of the excluded pupil, but the interests of their victims, if the offence involves treatment meted out to another pupil or, possibly, staff. Whilst, the principles of natural justice must continue to apply to the offending pupil, the head teacher must have regard to the interests of any victims, staff and the general school community. This is, again, covered fairly well in domestic legislation and guidance [see DfES Circular 10/99 and Education (Pupil Exclusions and Appeals) (Maintained Schools) (England) Regulations 2002, SI 2002/3178], but head teachers should be aware that a failure to exclude a pupil who had perpetuated a campaign of bullying and intimidation against a particular pupil or member of staff could, because the school will have a pro-active duty to protect those persons' rights under Article 3, lead to a claim from the victim if a further incident occurs because the offender has not been excluded. Given the press frenzy over decisions to reinstate, this may well be an important ground to be advanced if the offence relates to serious harassment or threatening behaviour against other pupils or staff which leads to school phobia or absence on stress grounds. A school's failure to deal with a pupil thief might also lead to a claim from the victim under Article 1 of the First Protocol – the right to property.

8.7.11 In all these cases, however, the victims' Convention Rights should not be seen as decisive, but as with all other elements of the investigation, a relevant factor to take into account when considering exercising the power to exclude.

8.7.12 Frequently disciplinary action and hence exclusion may arise where a pupil has made certain comments usually and quaintly referred to by head teachers as undermining their authority or discipline at a school. Telling a teacher to 'go f*** himself' is sadly too typical and some schools are more tolerant of swearing than others, possibly because in some schools if a school were to exclude every pupil who used the 'f' word they would have no pupils left and probably very few staff as well. On the other hand, pupils have also been disciplined for questioning a teacher's views in less forceful and offensive ways. In these cases, the Article 10 – freedom of expression – right may need to be considered.

8.7.13 Discrimination in the decision to exclude may also create Human Rights Act difficulties, albeit Article 14 only applies if a claimant can show that the discrimination occurs in respect of their exercise of another Convention Right. Thus if, as is probable, the right to education does not apply to an exclusion, unless freedom of expression, etc., can be invoked, the fact that there has been discrimination in the exclusion may not trigger any sanction under the Human Rights Act. However, as UK law is relatively rich in protective legislation against race, sex and disability discrimination (and since 1 September 2002 disability discrimination in respect of exclusions is now specifically unlawful), it is unlikely that Article 14 will add anything to these complaints. For example, in *R v Governors of McEntee School ex p Mbandaka* [[1999] EdCR 566], the judge commented that if there had been any substance in an allegation that there was racial discrimination in the disproportionate nature of an exclusion, he would have considered the exclusion to be unlawful.

8.7.14 Where it may be relevant, however, is in respect of discrimination which may potentially fall outside current UK law, the most obvious example of which may be discrimination on religious grounds, which falls outside the Race Relations Act 1976. There is no case law on this point, but where head teachers should be particularly wary, especially these days, might be in the case of, say, a Muslim pupil who expounds fundamentalism in the playground and incites fellow pupils to support terrorist groups fighting against the USA. Complaints are received from non-Muslim parents and staff. What should the head teacher do? 'Tread carefully' is probably the cowardly advice, but a head will need to ensure that in taking any action, he does respect, so far as he needs to, the right of pupil to express his views under Article 10. What expressions are appropriate will, in all cases, however, require the head to balance the pupil's rights against the qualifications set out in the Article [see 4.9.1*ff* above].

8. SCHOOL RULES, DISCIPLINE AND EXCLUSIONS

8.7.15 Once a child has been excluded, depending on the type of exclusion, the child's parent or the child if over 18, has certain domestic law rights to make representations to the school's pupil disciplinary committee and/ or an independent appeal panel arranged by the LEA which maintains the school [see s 52 Education Act 2002].

8.7.16 In the case of fixed term exclusions, there is no right of appeal as such to an independent appeal panel. If disability discrimination is alleged as being behind the exclusion, a claim may be brought to the SENDIST, but otherwise, the matter is dealt with in-school. Parents may make representations to the school's governing body in cases where the child has been excluded for five or more school days or where his exclusion would cause him to miss a public examination, but otherwise there are no express mechanisms for parents to raise concerns over the exclusion.

8.7.17 In the case of permanent exclusions, the school's pupil disciplinary committee will, first, decide whether or not to confirm the exclusion. The LEA is entitled to attend the meeting of the committee and make written or oral representations [s 66(2) SSFA 1998 and s 52 Education

Act 2002 and the associated regulations] as, obviously is the parent or, where appropriate, the excluded pupil.

8.7.18 Pupil disciplinary committees should comply with the guidance contained in DfEE Circular 10/99 (as amended from time to time whenever head teachers keep losing appeals). Such committees must also comply with the general principles of domestic administrative law such as allowing parents to have a fair hearing, the absence of bias and ensuring that the correct procedures are followed and relevant considerations are taken into account, etc.

8.7.19 They are nonetheless public authorities and must, therefore, act in ways which are compatible with the excluded pupil's, and any victim's, Convention Rights. Degrading treatment, freedom of expression, etc., may therefore be relevant. It is unlikely, however, that Article 6 – the right to a fair trial – will apply at this stage. This is for a number of reasons: first, *Simpson* appears to have decided that the 'right' to a school place is not a civil right which triggers Article 6 protection. Second, even if it was, because of the right to appeal [see 8.7.22 below] against the pupil discipline committee's decision to an independent appeal panel, the committee as such will not determine that right. And, third, the domestic case law has confirmed that any procedural errors at the committee level can be corrected by the independent appeal panel, which should look at all the merits of the exclusion afresh.

8.7.20 Again, however, the DfES at one stage appeared to be doing its best to prevent such a common sense approach. In one version of its guidance, it advised that an appeal panel should not direct reinstatement of a pupil simply because of procedural errors in earlier stages of the exclusion process. Possibly a reasonable view where procedural irregularities are minor, such as missed deadlines. If, however, there have been wholesale abuses of the procedure as required by the legislation and the guidance, such that they undermine the whole process, such as an inadequate or improper investigation of the offence, that may suggest that the whole process has been flawed and, if taken to court, could probably be overturned. If appeal panels are to have any role other than to rubber stamp the actions of head teachers, they must have the ability to take account of gross abuses in procedure, otherwise why have the procedure and how else will head teachers be held accountable? [At the time of finalising this text, the DfES had indicated that the new regulations dealing with exclusion appeals would prevent panels reinstating solely because of breach of the regulations. Such guidance does, fortunately, leave open the possibility that if there had been flagrant breaches of natural justice outside of the regulations, a panel could nonetheless reinstate. Those cases are hopefully, however, likely to be rare.]

8.7.21 Besides which, as will be seen, the courts have been reluctant to bring Article 6 into the appeal panel arena because they feel the domestic law provides sufficient safeguards. Take those away and the judiciary may have no alternative other than to intervene to protect excluded pupils.

8.7.22 After the pupil disciplinary process, then, if a pupil's permanent exclusion is upheld, the child's parent can appeal to an appeal panel under arrangements which must have been put in place by the LEA which maintains the school. The rules and procedures under which these panels operate are currently set out in Schedule 18 to the SSFA and in Circular 10/99 as amended [and in future will be contained in regulations under s 52 Education Act 2002]. The parties to the appeal are the parents and the school (through its pupil disciplinary committee, usually its chair). The head teacher is also entitled to attend, as are legal representatives for both parties and the excluded pupil. Victims should now be able to attend, if they wish, but it is the final player in this appeal which was felt to cause the biggest hindrance to the compatibility of these appeals with Article 6 of the Human Rights Act. Namely, the role of the LEA. Can an appeal hearing be, or even appear, independent and impartial when it is arranged, and the panel members are appointed, by one of the parties appearing before it, especially in cases where the LEA is seen to be supporting the school?

8.7.23 Arguably the point is, if *Simpson* is to prevail, academic. The panels do not determine civil rights, therefore issues of independence and impartiality are immaterial. (And even if this is wrong, as shall be seen, the courts have thought up a neat way round this, although one which probably will prove difficult to work in practice.)

8.7.24 Before going any further it is therefore necessary to examine the case of *Simpson* and see how apt it is to this process, which has, as Richards J pointed out, a potentially very serious impact on a child's education, his future employment and hence his whole life.

8.7.25 *Simpson v United Kingdom* [64 DR 188 (1989)] was determined back in 1989, arguably before the whole issue of pupil's rights reached the level it has in domestic law, and by the Commission, as opposed to the ECtHR itself, on a question of admissibility. It related to a child with SEN and concerned the rights of that child's mother to have him educated in a 'fee-paying special school' or a local comprehensive. He was not in any sense being denied education; that would be available, albeit not in the way his mother wanted at the local comprehensive.

8.7.26 The Commission concluded that in these circumstances, neither the 'right' such as it was under English law for a child to attend the school of his parent's preference nor the right not to be denied education under

Article 2 of the First Protocol, was of a civil nature for the purposes of Article 6. The Commission felt that 'for the purposes of the domestic law in question and the Convention, the right not to be denied elementary education falls, in the circumstances of the present case, squarely within the domain of public law, having no private law analogy and no repercussions on private rights or obligations'.

8.7.27 It therefore concluded that the rights in play under the then UK law relating to children with SEN and the right in play under Article 2 of the First Protocol, were not in the nature of private law rights. This raises the first question: are other rights under UK legislation equally incapable of being civil private law rights? In the case of places at schools, admissions and hence exclusions, probably not. They are statutory rights and duties. Interestingly, then, it would suggest that a child excluded from a private school where his or her rights are regulated by contract might be entitled to rely on Article 6 and have the right to a fair hearing, although, as has been seen [see 3.7.3*ff* above], his or her attempts could be thwarted on the basis that the private school was not a public authority; what though, if the child was placed there by an LEA or a local authority acting as a corporate parent – would the authority have an obligations to ensure that Article 6 compliant procedures were in place to address any decision of the private school to exclude? And here it may be appropriate to draw an analogy or at least seek assistance on the numerous cases at common law which have set out the circumstances in which an individual can seek to recover damages for breach of statutory as opposed to common law duties. For example, in *X v Bedfordshire County Council* [[1995] ELR 404] it was made clear that in the educational context it would be very rare for any one to be able to claim compensation in respect of a breach of statutory duty.

8.7.28 So, the conclusion was to be drawn that Article 6 was going to be of little relevance to the various committees and panels which considered appeals against exclusion. One area which did cause concern was the fact that the SSFA 1998 did not permit children excluded from pupil referral units to appeal against their exclusion. In response, the Secretary of State made provision for such appeals in the Education Act 2002 and has issued Regulations permitting children who had been excluded to appeal retrospectively for a period dating back to 1996 [see The Education (Pupil Referral Units) (Appeals Against Permanent Exclusion) (England) Regulations 2002, SI 2002/2550]. Similar Regulations have been issued by the National Assembly for Wales.

8.7.29 As also predicted, the whole exclusion process was one of the first aspects of school life considered by the Court of Appeal after the introduction of the Human Rights Act [*S, T, P v Brent LBC, Oxfordshire County Council, Head Teacher of Elliott School, the Secretary of State for Education and Skills and Others* [[2002] EWCA Civ 693]. This case involved a number of pupils excluded from different schools, all of whose exclusions had been upheld by independent appeal panels. The pupils challenged the decisions for a number of reasons, including the fact that the appeal panels were not sufficiently impartial and independent in the arrangements for their existence; that, even if they were, because they were obliged to have regard to advice from the Secretary of State, their independence and impartiality were unlawfully fettered and/or the role of the LEA gave rise to the appearance of bias.

8.7.30 In his judgment, as quoted above, Schiemann LJ emphasised the impact of exclusion on a child's education, though fell short of describing it as a fundamental right which activated Article 2 of the First Protocol. Analysing the role of appeal panels under the SSFA 1998, he acknowledged that that Act and its predecessors, had created 'a tribunal which has all the hallmarks of an independent adjudicative body. The Panels have the final say on a matter of critical importance to the pupil, school and society, and they are carefully constituted to ensure that they are independent of the school, the pupil and the LEA. One has only to read the scrupulous provisions about eligibility contained in the [Act] to see how central Parliament intended their independence and impartiality to be.' [*S, T, P v Brent LBC, Oxfordshire County Council, Head Teacher of Elliott School, the Secretary of State for Education and Skills and Others* [[2002] EWCA Civ 693 at paragraph 11]

8.7.31 In response to the challenge that these otherwise independent and impartial panels were fettered by the requirement that they should have regard to guidance issued by the Secretary of State, the Court acknowledged that the Panels have no presidential system or central direction, in contrast to, for example, the SENDIST. 'Instead, built into the constitution of appeal panels by s 68 [of the SSFA] is an obligation to have regard to any guidance issued by the Secretary of State', the effect of which is that 'appeal panels are required to act independently and decide impartially, but to do so in the light of the Secretary of State's guidance'.

8.7.32 Schiemann LJ did, however, impose an important proviso, and a very important one at that, given the Secretary of State's recent attempts to fetter the discretion of panels through such guidance: '…appeal panels, and schools too, must keep in mind that guidance is no more than that: it is not direction, and certainly not rules. Any Appeal Panel which, albeit on legal advice, treats the Secretary of State's Guidance as something to be strictly adhered to or simply follows it because it is there will be breaking its statutory remit in at least three ways: it will be failing to exercise its own judgment; it will be treating guidance as if it were rules; and it will, in lawyers' terms, be fettering its own discretion. Equally, however, it will be breaking its remit if it neglects the guidance.' Stating the somewhat obvious he then added, 'the task is not an easy one'.

8.7.33 If, it follows, appeal panels so act, the Court of Appeal clearly considers that they are Human Rights Act compliant. There are, however, a further three express or implied qualifications from the judgment which will also have to be met.

8.7.34 First, the Court of Appeal took what might be described as an innovative view of the role of the LEA in exclusion appeals. It is probably fair to say that in many cases, the LEA supports a school's decision to exclude and makes representations to that effect at an appeal. No more, or so it would appear.

> 'There is no question but that ... the LEA must maintain a completely objective stance....There is nothing wrong in the LEA informing the appeal panel of the situation in various schools in its area and providing other factual information. Self-evidently the school exclusions officer, or other limbs of the LEA, are likely to have information relevant to the issues which the appeal panel has to decide. But it is important to remember when considering the role of the LEA that we are here concerned with an appeal against a decision by the head teacher and the Discipline Panel to exclude a particular pupil, a decision against which Parliament has provided a right of appeal for the pupil to an independent body. It should be noted that Parliament has not provided a right of appeal for the LEA even if it considers that the head teacher should not have excluded the pupil. *It is no part of the function of the LEA to press for a particular conclusion in relation to a particular pupil. A clear instance would be a direct submission that the pupil ought or ought **not** to be permanently excluded* [at paragraph 24].'

8.7.35 Recognising that it could pose a difficult task for panels, Schiemann LJ recognised [at paragraph 25] that:

> 'The line between input and outcome is not always an easy one to draw, as any judge who has had to deal with expert evidence will know, and appeal panels need to be alert to the difference between the two. As often as not it will come down, not to interrupting or excluding extraneous submissions but to disregarding them; but panels must be careful not to let a point be reached where they appear to be acquiescing in an endeavour by the LEA – or by anyone else for that matter – to determine or influence their final

decision. It is here that a situation of ostensible bias is capable of developing unless the Panel halts it. ...*An example might be a submission by the LEA that the Panel's decision should not be such as to undermine the head teacher's authority: such a proposition, unobjectionable on the face of it, may readily be perceived as an attempt to uphold an exclusion on inadmissible grounds.*' [emphasis added as a rejoinder to all those head teachers who have recently tried to undermine the independence of the panel by asserting that any decisions overruling the head teacher's decision will undermine their authority].

8.7.36 Having examined the role of the appeal panel, the Secretary of State's guidance and the neutrality of the LEA, the Court returned to the question of whether the Human Rights Act and Article 6 were applicable [at paragraph 30]. As to the applicability of Article 6, Schiemann LJ felt that there were difficulties 'in the light of the present jurisprudence of the ECtHR in holding that a school exclusion appeal panel is a body which determines a pupil's civil rights, whether to education or reputation'. However, and the hint cannot be ignored, he went on,

'But let us make the perfectly tenable assumption that domestic human rights law, and arguably the ECtHR's jurisprudence too, will today regard at least the right not to be permanently excluded from school without good reason as a civil right for Article 6 purposes. Does the LEA's permitted role vis-à-vis the appeal panels then compromise the independence which Article 6 guarantees? Once that role is understood and restricted as the ordinary process of statutory construction requires, and as [the Court has spelt out in our judgment], the answer is no. Exactly the same is true of ministerial guidance: the possibility of its trenching on the independence and impartiality of appeal panels is negated by law because, for reasons we have given, the power to issue it is governed by the statutory purpose of creating and maintaining independent and impartial local tribunals.'

8.7.37 The conclusion that then perhaps might be reached is that:

1. Currently, exclusion appeal panels are not affected by Article 6 because they do not involve a dispute over a pupil's civil rights.

2. However, for any LEA or appeal panel to assume that therefore they can sit back and forget about that Article would be complacent and probably misguided. Schiemann LJ gave the clearest possible hint that he thought the point would not be far off when a court considered that Article 6 was engaged.

3. If that were to happen, it is likely that appeal panels, despite being arranged by the LEA and subject to ministerial guidance, could maintain sufficient independence and impartiality, provided that a number of safeguards were preserved or put in place.

4. These safeguards are, it is submitted that:

- The LEA's role must be neutral; it should provide information and not take sides.

- No LEA or school should try to argue impermissible grounds, such as that a decision to reinstate would undermine the head teacher's authority. (It may do, but Parliament clearly intended that there would be occasions when reinstatement should occur and that the undermining of a head's authority was a necessary price to pay.)

- Panels must have regard to guidance from the Secretary of State but they must not assume they are bound by it or must follow it religiously.

- And possibly a point implied from the decision rather than expressed – one of the key elements of the Court of Appeal's decision was their assumption that appeal panels had legal advisers (that may not necessarily be so – many LEAs use committee administrators or clerks with appropriate training). But, whatever the arrangements, where the panel's adviser is employed by the LEA or, even more so, if the legal adviser is in the same in-house legal department which also has service level agreements with the school and the LEA, it is not unforeseeable that a court could take exception and conclude, as might a reasonable parent, that this could taint the independence of the panel.

8.7.38 Qualifications therefore which are probably not too difficult to meet, provided, of course, that the Secretary of State does not impose new constitutions and provide guidance that undermine any of these key principles. [This book was written at the time when the then Secretary of State was proposing to issue new regulations under the Education Act 2002 altering the composition of panels to require teachers to be included on panels. She had also recently intervened in a case of an appeal panel's decision involving a Surrey school. There was a genuine concern that in appeasing the teachers' unions and sections of the tabloid press, the independence and impartiality and possibly the existence of these independent means of redress for wrongly excluded pupils could be compromised. However, at the time of finalising this book, the new Secretary of State had announced that the new regulations would alter the composition of panels but not to give head teachers a majority as originally envisaged. Instead, panels would have to comprise a lay member, a member who is a serving head teacher or who has been one within five years, and a governor of a maintained school or someone who has been one for a period of 12 months during the last five years. This will hopefully ensure that appeal panels continue to remain safe from challenge.] Requiring panels to include teachers who are employed by the LEA, as appears to be the case, in order to ensure appeal panels make decisions more favourable to head teachers, is hardly the best way to go about achieving this. Nor too, would be any further guidance which, contrary to the statements made by Schiemann LJ, effectively fetters the freedom of panels to reach a proper decision. Undermining school discipline is not, as he made clear, likely to be a valid ground. Parliament, by providing the statutory appeal mechanism, quite clearly intended that there would be occasions where children did have to be reinstated and, almost by definition, that will undermine the head teacher's decision.

8.7.39   The message therefore on exclusions, exclusion appeals and the Human Rights Act is very much: 'watch this space'.

9. Education Otherwise than at School

9.1   Two aspects of 'education otherwise' may raise Human Rights Act issues. First, there is the duty of an LEA to ensure that provision is made for children who are not at school [s 19 EA 1996] and, second, there are the rights of parents to educate their children at home free from interference from LEAs and the state.

9.2   S 19 of the EA 1996 provides that each local education authority shall make arrangements for the provision of suitable education at school or otherwise than at school for those children of compulsory school age who, by reason of illness, exclusion from school or otherwise, may not for any period receive suitable education unless such arrangements are made for them [s 19(1) EA 1996]. LEAs have similar powers in respect of young persons [s 19(4) EA 1996]. 'Suitable education' means efficient education suitable to a child's age, ability and aptitude and to any special educational needs he or she may have [s 19(6)].

9.3   Within the duty there are two aspects which caused concern under the 'old' domestic law and which could be affected by the Human Rights Act. First, a number of LEAs had been criticised for failing to keep track of children who were out of school and consequently for failing to make *any* provision for them. Second, where children had been identified, the provision could be patchy or limited and frequently affected by the lack of resources available to the LEA for this type of provision.

9.4   The latter point was considered by the House of Lords in *R v East Sussex County Council ex p Tandy* [[1998] ELR 251], where it was held that the lack of resources argument could not excuse a failure to provide education to meet a child's needs. S 19, the House of Lords held, imposed a duty in respect of each individual child and what constituted suitable education for that child depended on the specific educational considerations relevant to him or her; the resources available to the LEA, or the lack of them, was not a relevant factor.

9.5   The adequacy of the provision available for these children has also been tightened up through DfES guidance so that from 1 September 2002 LEAs are expected to provide five hours tuition a day for children who are out of school, specifically excluded children [*Social Exclusion: The LEA Role in Pupil Support* DfES Circular 11/99, paragraph 5.18].

9.6   If LEAs fail to provide this, is it a breach of the Human Rights Act? Potentially, it is, as well as being a breach of s 19. This is because the right to education in Article 2 of the First Protocol has been held to include a right to an *effective* education [see *The Belgian Linguistics Case* (1979-1980) 1 EHRR 252 and 5.2.6 above]. If DfES guidance is that an effective education for children out of school can be provided only if they receive x hours tuition otherwise than in a school per week, it would be hard for an LEA to defend its failure if challenged on the basis of Article 2 of the First Protocol.

9.7   The second aspect of the LEA's s 19 duty is perhaps the most important of all: ensuring that all children for whom it is responsible are identified and either suitable education provided by the LEA or, where parents have made the deliberate choice to educate their children at home, that such education is monitored to ensure it is suitable.

9.8   Here, if an LEA fails to appreciate that a child is in its area and out of school, or having had that child brought to its attention it does nothing to ensure that he or she is receiving suitable education, it is not too fanciful to suggest that that LEA would be in breach of Article 2 of the First Protocol as, patently, that child would be denied his right to education. LEAs must have a positive duty in these cases to protect children, even if their parents are the reason why they are not attending school [see also 7.2.16*ff* above]. Hence LEAs will need to have adequate measures in place to ensure that they know the children for whom they are responsible, know which children have been excluded from school, that they are not just left to drop out of the system, and that their education welfare officers do take steps, even where parents are obstructive, to enforce the attendance obligations.

9.
EDUCATION
OTHERWISE
THAN AT SCHOOL

9.9   In contrast, the second Human Rights Act point relates to the rights of parents to 'do their own thing' without intervention from LEAs. The choice to educate a child at home, rather than in the state or independent sector, is probably a philosophical conviction within the second limb of Article 2 of the First Protocol, where the parents believe sincerely that they can provide a better education for their children [see, for example, *The Lord is my headmaster – Christian evangelists are shunning local schools and educating their children at home because they believe that the schools are spreading lies, The Independent*, 10 November 2002]. Indeed, domestic law has always recognised the right of parents to educate their children at home, provided that the education provided is suitable to the child's educational needs. That right is probably strengthened by the Human Rights Act, but the point where the Human Rights Act may lead to conflict concerns the LEA's rights or powers to monitor the parents' provision to ensure that it is suitable.

9.10   The potential for Article 8 – the right to respect for one's private and family life – to be invoked to prevent monitoring has already been considered in the context school attendance orders [see 7.2.18*ff* above] and those points are as relevant here. *Prima facie*, efforts by an LEA to inspect home-based provision will infringe Article 8 and possibly Article 1 of the First Protocol – the right to peaceful enjoyment of property.

9.11   As discussed at 7.2.20, the LEA could not force their way in as they have no statutory right of entry, so that sort of interference would not be 'in accordance with the law' and hence the qualifications to Article 8 could not be applied. Article 8 may therefore well prevent an LEA requiring a parent to show it what provision was being made. This is not, however, the same as saying that this could, in effect, permit an obstructive parent to prevent an LEA ever proceeding to issue a school attendance order. The reason is that s 437 places the onus on the parent to satisfy the LEA that the provision is suitable. If the parent does not tell the LEA what he or she is doing or refuses to allow the LEA to see, it is hard to say that the LEA can ever be satisfied. Indeed, it might be acting improperly if it did say it was satisfied without considering the provision. Thus, if the parent cannot satisfy the LEA, the LEA is obliged to proceed to the next stage and serve notice on the parent of its intent to serve a school attendance order [s 438 EA 1996]. Article 8 rights may therefore merely have academic interest in this process.

9.   EDUCATION OTHERWISE THAN AT SCHOOL

9.12   Similarly, Article 1 of the First Protocol may well be infringed if an LEA were to force its way in to monitor home provision. Having an LEA inspector appear on the doorstep could well amount to an interference with the parent's peaceful enjoyment of their property. Again, because the LEA does not have the power of entry, the qualifications to permit the LEA to interfere will not be met. However, as with Article 8, this Convention Right becomes, in some senses, academic, as the LEA could simply argue that unless and until the parents prove to them that the child is receiving suitable education, the LEA can take enforcement steps anyway. So, whilst a refusal to allow them entry to the parental home may be permissible, it will not prevent the LEA taking the necessary action to ensure that the child is protected.

9.13   Consequently, it is hoped that UK law is already sufficiently stringent in this regard as to the duties imposed on LEAs and that the coming into force of the Human Rights Act is unlikely to add much, if anything, to these obligations.

10. Special Educational Needs

10.1 Introduction

10.1.1 The area of special educational needs, given its history of confrontation and litigation, would perhaps have suggested itself as an area in which the Human Rights Act would have a significant impact. Instead, ironically, due largely to that history of litigation which has seen many challenges taken to Europe and fail, it has been surprisingly unaffected and, where challenges have been brought in the UK courts, the domestic law has, so far, withstood much of the judicial scrutiny.

10.1.2 Another factor may well be that because of the campaigning litigation of the last twenty years, UK law has already been reformed to a point where it has been pressured into becoming compatible in any event. Examples such as the change from local appeal committees to the truly independent SEN and Disability Tribunal, the extension of parents' appeal rights and even the acceptance that causes of action may exist permitting individuals to sue if an LEA or school fails to detect needs are all changes which, if they had not already occurred, might have been forced by the Human Rights Act.

10.2 Simpson

10.2.1 Nonetheless, in principle, the Human Rights Act is unlikely to add much to the UK law. This is again due to the old and probably rightly battered, but nonetheless still surviving, decision of the European Commission in the *Simpson* [(1989) 64 D & R 188] case. The claim in this case concerned a child with dyslexia. His original LEA issued a statement of SEN for him naming a private fee-paying special school. His parents then moved into the area of another LEA which reviewed the statement, amended it and proposed that he should attend a local comprehensive school. The boy's mother appealed (under the then existing appellate system) to both a local appeal committee and then the Secretary of State, but without success. She then took her case to the European Commission on a number of grounds:

1. That the appeal mechanism in place breached Article 6 as it was biased, the appeal at local level was to the authority against which the appeal was being made (since remedied anyway with the introduction of the SENT, now SENDIST); it was not speedy;

there was no fair or oral hearing before the Secretary of State; financial restraints placed on LEAs by central Government meant there was institutional bias against a full and fair consideration of a child's SEN which might result in public expense; and that the child's mother did not have sufficient means to challenge the Secretary of State's decision by judicial review but was not so poor as to qualify for legal aid.

2. That the child had been denied the right to education (under Article 2 of the First Protocol) in accordance with his educational needs or in accordance with his mother's philosophical convictions; and

3. That to place him in a comprehensive school would lead to a deterioration in his mental condition and his ability to be educated, which would be a breach of his rights under Article 8.

10.2.2 The claim was dismissed by the Commission on the basis that there was no dispute over a civil right.

'The various Education Acts have created obligations on local education authorities to provide suitable education for all children in their areas. Parents dissatisfied with the education proposed for their children may complain to the Secretary of State and, ultimately, they may seek judicial review of the decisions of the local authority or Minister. Thereby the relevant legislation has created a right which reflects the guarantes of Article 2 of Protocol No. 1 to the Convention – a right for children not to be denied an education appropriate to their needs and aptitudes.'

10.2.3 Nor did the Commission consider the claim to relate to a 'civil' right:

'The Commission considers that for the purposes of the domestic law in question and the Convention, the right not to be denied elementary education falls, in the circumstances of the present case, squarely within the domain of public law, having no private law analogy and no repercussions on private rights or obligations.'

10.2.4 The claim that his mother's philosophical convictions had been infringed was defeated on the technical ground that she should have claimed herself and the Commission could not entertain claims brought on behalf of another. As to the boy's claim under Article 2 of the First Protocol, the Commission observed that 'it was not an absolute right which requires Contracting Parties to subsidise private education of a particular type or level. In principle, it guarantees access to public educational facilities which have been created at a given time and the possibility of drawing benefit from the education received.' This right 'by its very nature calls for regulation by the State, regulation which

10.
SPECIAL
EDUCATIONAL
NEEDS

may vary in time and place according to the needs and resources of the community and of individuals', as long as the substance of the right to education is preserved'. The Commission noted that the UK Government provided 'special education for disabled children either in normal mainstream schools with special departments, or in specialised segregated institutions. In keeping with current educational trends, s 2 of the Education Act 1981 provides that children with special educational needs should be educated in an ordinary school with normal children of their own age if that is compatible with the special education which the former require, the provision of efficient education for other children at the school and the efficient use of resources. The Commission recognises that there must be a wide measure of discretion left to the appropriate authorities as to how to make the best use possible of the resources available to them in the interests of disabled children generally. While these authorities must place weight on parents' and pupils' views, it cannot be said that the first sentence of Article 2 of Protocol No. 1 requires the placing of a dyslexic child in a private specialised school, with the fees paid by the State, when a place is available in an ordinary State school which has special teaching facilities for disabled children.'

10.2.5 Finally, as to the claim that sending the boy to a comprehensive would infringe his private or family life or the integrity of his person, the Commission found that the claim was only hypothetical as the child had never attended the school and could not therefore prove deterioration in his mental condition.

10.2.6 *Simpson* is therefore an important case which probably cuts off most claims under the Human Rights Act, certainly in respect of the ability of a parent to request that their child go to a non-maintained special school and compel an LEA to fund it. That decision was embedded further by the subsequent decision of the European Commission in *SP v United Kingdom* [Application No 28915/95, 17 January 1997]. Here, another dyslexic child had complained that there had been a violation of his right to education because teaching staff at two maintained schools and two independent schools he attended had failed to take account of and address his SEN and because an LEA had refused his mother's request for a statutory assessment.

10.2.7 The Commission felt that after looking at the steps taken by the LEA, it could not criticise the LEA for refusing the request for the assessment and recognised 'that there must be a wide measure of discretion left to the appropriate authorities as to how to make the best use possible of the resources available to them in the interests of disabled children generally'. It also abruptly and succinctly dismissed the claim that the schools had failed to address the child's needs: 'With regard to the criticisms made of the various teaching that the applicant has received in his four schools he has attended, it is not the Commission's task to assess the standard of teaching provided by schools.' It is also now arguable that the latter point is adequately covered by the UK courts recognising the ability of pupils to claim compensation for negligent detection and remedying of their SEN [see, *X v Bedfordshire County Council* [1995] 2 AC 633, [1995] ELR 404, HL*; Phelps v Hillingdon* [2001] 2AC 619, [2000] ELR 499, HL].

10.2.8 So what aspects of the SEN regime might therefore be susceptible to challenge under the Human Rights Act?

10.3 Placement

10.3.1 One aspect which was thought might cause difficulties was the ability of LEAs to name a residential placement and, in effect, force a child to live away from his home. Given though that many parents seek to require LEAs to send their children to an independent or non-maintained special school and, more importantly, pay for it, the obverse could also have been relevant so far as the children are concerned: could an LEA resist a parent's representations that their child should attend such a school on the basis that the LEA, even if the parents were not, was protecting the child's right to family life, even if the parents didn't necessarily want him or her?

10.3.2 Surprisingly it took two years for the point to be raised in an appeal to the High Court against a decision of the SENT. In *CB v Merton LBC and SENT* [[2002] EWHC 877 (Admin), [2002] ELR 441], the LEA had named a non-maintained special school in the child's statement of SEN. As that was far from the family home the child had to board. There were also a number of issues about the parents' care for their child which suggested a residential placement was appropriate. The parents, however, wanted their child to attend a local day school. The LEA's decision was upheld on appeal to the SENT and the parents appealed, arguing that the SENT's decision to name the residential school contrary to the wishes of the mother and the child himself was in breach of Article 8 – the right to respect for their private and family life – the interference being with one of the fundamental elements of family life, the mutual enjoyment by parent and child of each other's company. The point was also made that the Tribunal's decision was the start of a process of enforcement which could, if the parents did not ensure their child attended the named school, lead to prosecution under s 444 of the Education Act 1996.

10.3.3 Article 8 is, it should be remembered, a qualified right so interference could be justified if it was in accordance with the law, was necessary in a democratic society in the interests of, amongst others, the protection of public health and morals and the protection of the rights and freedoms of others, and is proportionate. In *CB* there was no argument that the placement was not in accordance with the law and was not necessary. The judge concluded that any interference was perfectly justified by all the factors in the case. However, he also went on to consider whether the Tribunal's decision could amount to an interference with the child's Article 8 right in any event and found that it could not. The judge accepted that an order requiring a child to attend a residential school was *prima facie* an interference with family life that required justification under Article 8. But, he held, that was not the effect of the Tribunal's decision. The SENT's decision instead had the effect of requiring the LEA to name a particular school in a statement of SEN; it was then for the LEA to decide whether a school attendance order should be served to compel the child's attendance at that school (which, of course, must be named in the order if it is named in the statement) and for the order to be enforced through the magistrates court. It would not therefore be the decision to name the school which would expose the mother to prosecution, but the mother's failure to ensure the child attended that school and/or received suitable etc education.

10.3.4 The decision therefore suggests that the naming of a residential school is not, in itself, capable of amounting to an interference with either a parent's or child's Article 8 right. The decision is not, however, that clear and Sullivan J was obviously concerned to achieve the right result for the child by ensuring he attended the appropriate school for him despite his mother's views. He therefore suggested that a decision by the SENT to name a school (and presumably the earlier decision by the LEA to do the same) did not *require* the child to attend the school. The mother could have allowed him to attend the school or made alternative arrangements and the only requirement would be, effectively, any subsequent enforcement action for non-attendance. This raises a number of issues. First, the act of naming the school in the statement is the first stage on the route to compelling an unwilling mother to send her child to that school and, second, the court appears to have overlooked the fact that a school *must*, once named in a statement, normally be the *only school* which can be named in a subsequent school attendance order. The ingenuity of the decision was, however, the distinction the judge made between naming the school and taking the action which would effectively interfere with family rights.

10.3.5 It seems likely that the courts will hold that a decision to name a residential school contrary to a parent and/or child's wishes will not be an interference for the purpose of Article 8. Where the Article 8 issue may arise, however, is if enforcement action is taken against the reluctant parent and that is considered in more detail in Chapter 7 above.

10.3.6 Even if there is an actual interference at the point at which the school is named, it is likely that there will be very few cases when a properly reasoned decision to place a child in residential provision where, after proper and adequate investigation, there was no alternative non-residential provision would fail to meet one of the qualifications in Article 8(2) justifying interference in any event. This was recognised by Sullivan J, who held on the fact that the child would not have his needs met unless he attended the specialist residential school both the LEA and SENT had named.

10.3.7 So, residential provision should not be in breach of Article 8. What, though, of the converse situations where either the parent insists their child should be placed at residential school over the LEA's option of a day school or where the parents insist their child should be educated at home (the consequential question of whether parents can object to an LEA checking up on the provisions being made for a child at home is considered in Chapter 7).

10.3.8 With the former, it seems difficult to envisage a situation where a parent's demands that their child be educated at a residential school promotes private or family life. The exception might be if there is an allegation that the child has been bullied at his or her local day school, the LEA and the SENT, as public authorities, having a responsibility to protect the physical integrity of the child. In fact, in many cases an LEA might be able to argue on behalf of the child that the parent's insistence that the child attends a residential placement, if not strictly necessary to meet the child's needs, could itself be an infringement of the child's Article 8 rights. And remember, public authorities are under a positive obligation to protect such rights.

10. SPECIAL EDUCATIONAL NEEDS

10.4 Home-based education

10.4.1 Home education, however, is a slightly different story and also involves issues relating to the inspection of the parent's provision, which is considered in more detail in Chapter 7 on school attendance. In the SEN context, the question of home-based, usually Lovaas, provision, tends to be the issue which currently causes most disputes.

10.4.2 Under the EA 1996, parents can make representations that their child should receive such support; it is not an expression which, *prima facie*, an LEA is required to meet [see s 9 and paragraph 3 of Schedule 27 to the 1996 Act and *Inclusive Schooling: Children with Special Educational Needs*, DfES/0774/2001]. The LEA has the power to make such provision under s 319 of the EA 1996 but only if it is satisfied that it would be inappropriate for the child's required special educational provision to be made in a school [s 319(1) and see *T v SENT and Wiltshire County Council* [2002] EWHC 1474 (Admin)].

10.4.3 In *T v SENT and Wiltshire County Council* [[2002] EWHC 1474 (Admin)], parents wished their child to receive Lovaas provision paid for by the LEA. It was argued that their belief that the Lovaas programme was essential to their child's development and eventual integration into mainstream education was a philosophical conviction within the second limb of Article 2 of the First Protocol. If so, both the LEA and the SENT on appeal should have given weight to that conviction and taken it into account when considering the force of the parental representations. That argument was rejected. On the facts, the SENT had concluded that a school would have been appropriate to make the required provision and so the SENT was prohibited by s 319 from naming Lovaas provision in any event. On the human rights point, however, the judge concluded that the parents' preference for the programme did not amount to a conviction. He concluded that the reasons for the parents' preference for the Lovaas programme rested on a judgment that such a programme was more likely to meet their child's SEN and to enable him to be integrated effectively into mainstream schooling (and, in fact, the father was committed to the principle of inclusive schooling). That, according to Richards J, fell far short of a philosophical conviction in favour of the Lovaas programme. So, it would be fair to assume, a belief in the effectiveness of a particular type of programme or provision will not amount to a philosophical conviction.

10.4.4 The final issue which concerns home education in the SEN context may arise as more LEAs introduce programmes which tend to recognise the need for some home based intervention. In most cases, parents may welcome such an approach, but what if some are adamantly against such a programme and refuse to allow the LEA tutors into their home on the grounds that their entry would infringe their Article 8 rights to a private and family life? An LEA could not force their way in and, if the parents were providing alternative suitable education, there would be no possibility of enforcement action being taken. If an LEA knew the parents would refuse to co-operate, could it nonetheless go ahead and name their programme and could the SENDIST uphold that on appeal, knowing that what they were ordering was incapable of implementation? Decisions such as *Sunderland City Council v P and* C [[1996] ELR 283] suggest that perhaps they cannot; the analogy being that if a school cannot legally take a child, the SENDIST cannot name it – if parents refuse to permit tutors to enter their home, the SENDIST could not name that either, as the provision would appear impossible to implement. However, that could deprive a child of the most appropriate education and the better view can perhaps now be supported by the decision in *CB*. In effect, in *CB*, the judge held that, if Article 8 rights existed, they would not be infringed by the act of naming provision in a statement; i.e. the naming was facilitative, not executive. That may still leave open the problem of what happens further down the line, if parents still refuse to comply, but it would seem that the parents' assertion of Article 8 rights should not, in itself, prevent an LEA's home-based provision being named in a Statement.

10.4.5 Inspection of home-based provision has been considered in Chapters 7 and 9.

10.4.6 Placement and the content of a statement of SEN are probably the areas which may cause most human rights problems in the SEN field. If one was trying to predict where else they might crop up, the tendency would be to think of appeals, the rights of the child in the process and the consequences of a failure on the part of a school or LEA to spot or deal with a child's SEN.

10.5 Appeals and compensation

10.5.1 As a consequence of the introduction of the SENT (now SENDIST) in the 1993 Education Act, any challenges to the appeal system on the grounds that it lacks independence and impartiality are most probably doomed to failure. Even if there was still some underlying concern about a tribunal of that nature, organised by a Government department responsible generally and nationally for issues which could be considered in appeals, our old friend *Simpson* probably provides sufficient justification to leave the system just the way it is. After all, even though organised within the aegis of the DfES, the SENDIST Tribunal does enjoy a certain amount of autonomy, the chairmen are appointed by another department (that of the Lord Chancellor) and, unlike the case involving the Employment Tribunals and claims against the DTI [see, for example, *Scanfuture United Kingdom Ltd v Secretary of State for Trade and Industry* [2001] IRLR 416, EAT], the Government department will never be a party to an appeal as such.

10.5.2 The only lingering doubt, should *Simpson* subsequently be held not to apply, is the question of public funding for parents and whether the lack of its availability could infringe Article 6. Assuming that S*impson* is wrong and civil rights are in play in an appeal to the SENDIST, one of the principles inherent in the right to a fair trial is that a party's access to a court or tribunal should not be unfairly restricted. If a parent is unable to obtain public funding, can the tribunal hearing be fair? In

Faulkner (Ian) v United Kingdom [Application No 30308/96 1 December 1998], the Commission found the UK Government to be in breach of Article 6 because legal aid was unavailable in Guernsey to enable the claimant to bring civil legal proceedings for false imprisonment. The Commission was satisfied that the claimant required legal representation and that his financial circumstances prevented that. He therefore could not effectively achieve access to the courts to determine his civil rights.

10.5.3 Whether the courts in the UK will, however, interpret *Faulkner* as saying that everyone should be entitled to legal aid or public funding is debatable, Indeed, surprisingly there have been few such challenges since October 2000. In any event, given the nature of SENDIST and its procedures, it is difficult to say that a parent will be denied access to the Tribunal simply because they are unable to afford legal representation when there are a number of charities available to assist and the Tribunal itself discourages legal representation.

10.5.4 Until the 1993 Education Act, the rights of appeal open to parents of children with SEN were limited. After that Act, however, the rights of appeal were extended and have been further extended by the amendments resulting from the Special Educational Needs and Disability Act 2001. There are, however, still a couple of areas where rights of appeal are denied, and where conceivably human rights issues could arise. In particular, it is still the case that a parent cannot appeal to SENDIST against the decision of an LEA to carry out an assessment or re-assessment of their child's needs under s 323 of the EA 1996; the description of the non-educational need and provision contained in a Statement; or against the refusal of a health or social services authority to provide assistance under s 322 of the EA 1996.

10.5.5 The first of these – no appeal against a decision to assess – is probably human rights compatible. At this stage the LEA are not determining the parents' or child's civil rights so Article 6 is not an issue; if there can be no interference with Article 8, privacy rights when a school is named [see *CB*], the mere act of initiating an assessment can also hardly be considered as an interference with a person's right to privacy; and, even if there was, the social imperative in ensuring children's needs are identified and met should provide justification for any interference caused by an assessment. The lack of rights of appeal in the other two cases is also unlikely to raise human rights issues for similar reasons.

10.5.6 Another principle which the Strasbourg case law has identified as forming part of the right to a fair trial is the importance, for a trial to be effective, of the ability of the court to enforce its decisions [see *Hornsby v Greece* (1997) 24 EHRR 250]. Until the Special Educational Needs and Disability Act 2001, there was a general problem with SENT orders being complied with by LEAs and the lack of any means for the Tribunal to enforce its decisions. However, with the introduction of s 336A of the EA 1996 and the express duty imposed on LEAs to comply with tribunal orders within prescribed times, that problem should have disappeared.

10.5.7 A further concern to parents groups and those representing children was the apparent lack of involvement on the part of the child. Again, as we have seen [see Chapter 6], the legislation is based on the presumption that a child lacks capacity and that the parent should be charged with protecting his or her rights. In some cases, this could easily be disputed, but it is an explanation for the fact that it was the parent who was consulted, notified, etc. as to the assessment process and who could appeal. That is still the case, although both the 2001 Code of Practice and the Special Educational Needs Tribunal Regulations 2001 have strived to secure a greater involvement on the part of the child wherever practical. There is also provision for a foster parent or social services department to take those decisions and appeal on a child's behalf which should protect the seriously 'neglected' child in care. What none of this addresses, though, is the child who is not in care but whose parents do not care too much about his or her welfare to ensure that he or she is assessed and/or receives the appropriate provision. There is also the issue that a parent might seek a placement which the child does not want or which may not be beneficial. Again, on appeal, the fact that the child does now have greater involvement may assist but it still does not get round the problem of the child whose parents fail him or her. Maybe there will never be a solution to that problem, but a child still cannot appeal in his or her own right. Presumably *Simpson* saves that from being a problem under the Human Rights Act and it may therefore be an issue which needs to await a wholesale review of the rights of children in UK law.

10.
SPECIAL
EDUCATIONAL
NEEDS

10.5.8 Finally, does the Human Rights Act have any impact on schools or LEAs which are alleged to have failed to identify, assess and make provision to meet a child's SEN? Again, probably not, as, since the cases of *X v Bedfordshire County Council* and *Phelps v Hillingdon LBC* [[1995] 2 AC 633, [1995] ELR 404, HL; and [2001] 2AC 619, [2000] ELR 499, HL supra], domestic law has recognised that duties of care exist and that remedies can be sought in the event of failure on the part of the public authorities.

10.5.9 In any event, the Commission gave the clearest possible indication in *SP v United Kingdom* [Application No 28915/95 17 January 1997] that such claims would not invoke the right to education. In that case, the claimant complained that his school teachers had failed to take account of his special needs which prevented him deriving a positive benefit from his education and contributed to his behavioural, emotional and social problems. There was also a complaint that the LEA had failed to make an assessment of his needs. This, it was claimed, amounted to a denial of his right to education under Article 2 of the First Protocol. The Commission thought otherwise and held that, on the facts, the LEA had acted properly and could not be criticised for refusing to carry out an assessment. It recognised that the appropriate authorities should be given a wide element of discretion as to how best to make use of the resources available to them in the interest of disabled children generally. It also considered that it was not its role to assess the standard of teaching provided in schools. Whether the same decision would have been made if the Commission had felt that the LEA had acted wrongly is debatable, but even so, the suggestion from the decision is that as long as the substance of the right to education is preserved, even negligently, there will be no breach of Article 2 of the First Protocol.

10.5.10 Where the Human Rights Act might have an impact is on the technical process of dealing with these claims. In *X v Bedfordshire County Council*, in the LEA cases the LEAs had sought to have the claims 'struck out', i.e. dismissed by the courts without the need for a trial on the basis that in law they had no chance of success. As it happened, the House of Lords considered that they did have a chance of success but, also, in pre-Human Rights Act times, the House indicated its concern that striking out was the not the way to deal with these cases. In so indicating, as other courts had previously and have subsequently done [see, for example *Barrett v Enfield LBC* [1999] 3 WLR 79], the House of Lords was reflecting European jurisprudence that considered that the ability to strike out a case without hearing the totality of a claim could amount to a breach of Article 6 – the right to a fair trial [see, for example, *Osman v United Kingdom* (1998) 5 BHRC 382 and *Barrett* supra].

10.5.11 If, however, courts permit a claim to be brought, the typical education malpractice or failure to educate claims are unlikely to raise issues under the right to education.

10.
SPECIAL
EDUCATIONAL
NEEDS

11. Curriculum

11.1 Introduction

11.1.1 The impact of the Human Rights Act on the curriculum is likely to be minimal. The ECtHR has frequently concluded that the content of education and the quality of its provision are matters for the individual state and are areas in which the ECtHR should tread warily [see, for example, *SP v United Kingdom* Application 28915/95 17 January 1997 and *Kjeldsen, Busk Madsen and Pedersen v Denmark* (1976) 1 EHRR 711].

11.1.2 It is equally likely that domestic courts will be unwilling to intervene in such matters, preferring to leave them to schools and the politicians who establish the curricular parameters, granting them considerable deference.

11.2 National C urriculum

11.2.1 Schools and LEAs must operate within the framework of the National Curriculum, which is now contained in Part 6 of the Education Act 2002 [previously Part V of the EA 1996].

11.2.2 Although the content of the curriculum is something to which courts will grant judicial deference [see 3.12.4*ff* above], certain standards will be required. First, the quality of the education provided through the curriculum must reach a minimum standard [*The Belgian Linguistics Case* (1979-80) 1 EHRR 252] in order for the education to be effective. Second, the curriculum should be a means of ensuring plurality and must not be a means by which one view is advanced or pupils are indoctrinated; the information or knowledge imparted must be conveyed in an objective, critical and pluralist manner [*Kjeldsen, Busk Madsen and Pedersen v Denmark* (1976) 1 EHRR 711].

11.2.3 Here, UK law should be Convention compliant and particularly, having regard to the concern about political indoctrination, s 406 EA 1996 provides that the teaching of any subject cannot promote partisan political views. It also ensures in junior [i.e. in the United Kingdom, primary] schools that the pursuit of partisan political activities by registered pupils is forbidden. Section 407 then places a duty on LEAs,

11.
CURRICULUM

governing bodies and head teachers to take 'reasonably practicable' steps to ensure that, when political issues are discussed, pupils are provided with a balanced presentation of opposing views.

11.3 Sex education

11.3.1 This does then raise the issue of 'Section 28' and the misunderstanding in schools as to what can or cannot be taught about homosexuality or sexual orientation. Section 28 of the Local Government Act 1998, which inserted s 2A into the Local Government Act 1986 [so it should be known as Section 2A anyway] prohibits the intentional promotion of homosexuality and the promotion of the teaching of the acceptability of homosexuality as a pretended family relationship in maintained schools by local authorities. It does not, and despite the confusion, never has, prevented schools teaching about homosexuality or dealing with homophobic abuse [see *Pearce v Governing Body of Mayfield School* [[2001] EWCA Civ 1347]. For that reason, it may not cause any problems vis-à-vis the Human Rights Act, as a school is not prevented from providing an informed and balanced discussion of the subject. If it were, however, to be read as preventing teaching about, as opposed to simply banning proselytising in favour of, sexual orientation, that will not necessarily bring it into conflict with any provision of the Human Rights Act, although its compatibility with Articles 8, 10, 12 and 14 has long been questioned.

11.3.2 Given the emotions aroused by Section 28, it is perhaps not surprising that complaints about sex education have been raised in the ECtHR. However, UK law has provided certain protections so a parent can ask that his or her child be excused wholly or partly from receiving sex education at a maintained school, so long as the education does not form part of the National Curriculum, where such withdrawal is not permitted [s 405 EA 1996]. Whether the child always wants this, or benefits from being excluded, is perhaps debatable and just another example of how UK law gives rights to parents, not to children.

11.3.3 Nevertheless, in countries which have encouraged a greater openness and concern that children should receive sex education, the ECtHR has been unwilling to permit parents to prevent their children being exposed to such teaching. Compulsory sex education does not therefore violate Article 2 of the First Protocol [*Kjeldsen, Busk Madsen and Pedersen v Denmark* (1976) 1 EHRR 711]. A school must, however, ensure that 'carelessness, lack of judgement or misplaced proselytism' by any teacher who provides the education does not exceed the public interest pursued by such education. The education must also not be aimed at advocating a particular kind of sexual behaviour (pluralism here, too, is apparently important) nor encouraging precocious or promiscuous behaviour or practices that are dangerous to health or which parents may consider reprehensible.

11.4   Religious education

11.4.1   Under domestic law, all pupils at maintained schools must have religious education provided for them [s 80 Education Act 2002] and there must be at least one act of daily collective worship [s 70 SSFA 1998].

11.4.2   These provisions are, however, Human Rights Act compliant because domestic law enables parent's religious convictions (though not philosophical convictions) to be respected by permitting them to ask that their child be withdrawn wholly or partly from religious education and/ or collective worship [s 71 SSFA 1998]. Thus, whilst a parent cannot demand alternative provision, this provision should ensure compatibility with Article 2 of the First Protocol.

11.
CURRICULUM

12. Parents' Rights

12.1 Introduction

12.1.1 Throughout this work we have effectively considered the rights of parents under the Human Rights Act in respect of their children's education. The education legislation in England and Wales is very much geared up (whether correctly or not, will be considered in Chapter 13) to enabling parents to make representations, express their convictions or be involved in their children's education.

12.1.2 Hopefully, areas where parents may be prevented unlawfully from having their convictions considered have been identified (for example by being prevented from expressing their religious or philosophical convictions on an application for admission [see *6.3.3ff* above and *R (on the application of K) v Newham LBC* [2002] EWHC 405 (Admin)] and will not be repeated here.

12.2 Preventing parents entering schools

12.2.1 One area which has not been considered elsewhere is the right of a parent to enter the school which their child attends. In the majority of cases this does not cause a problem as parents are willing to cooperate as to when they can visit the school and whilst there behave in a reasonable manner.

12.2.2 The problem might arise in the case of a parent who does not behave reasonably, visits the school when they want and/or is abusive to staff when they do enter. Does this have any Human Rights Act implications?

12.2.3 Again, the answer is probably not as the Convention Rights do not provide a positive right to parents to enter their children's schools and, in any event, domestic law has provided clarification as to when and how parents may enter and be excluded from school sites [*Wandsworth LBC v A* [2000] EdCR 167].

12.2.4 Before 2000, it was assumed that parents had no more than a bare licence to enter school premises and this could be revoked if they behaved unreasonably. After the *Wandsworth* case, though, whilst parents have no licence to roam at will, enter classrooms during lessons or interfere with the teaching being provided, they have more than a bare licence to enter their child's school. A parent thus has a considerable interest in being able to visit their child's school (even greater than that of a person using other local authority premises such as a library or recreation ground) and consequently, before they could be banned from the site, the head teacher had an obligation to give the parent an opportunity to make representations. Although not suggesting that a head teacher had to conduct a formal investigation or hold a formal hearing, the Court of Appeal found that a head teacher should have outlined his allegations to the parent and then invited their comments (which presumably would be more polite than the comments which led to the head teacher considering banning them in the first place).

12.2.5　This does seem a sensible approach and one which would meet Article 6, assuming that the ban from the school site does determine the parent's civil rights. If, as the Court of Appeal indicated, the parent does have some legal right to come into school, it may well do so, although provided head teachers follow the simple process laid down by the Court of Appeal there should be no Human Rights Act compatibility issues.

12.2.6　That being the case there should also be no problems with the criminal offence available to deal with persons (including parents) causing a nuisance or disturbance on school premises contrary to s 547 EA 1996 as amended by Schedule 20 of the Education Act 2002. Such offences are tried before a magistrates court (providing the independent and impartial tribunal) and the offence is not one of strict liability so avoiding the potential problems of non-attendance prosecutions [see Chapter 7].

12.3　Parental rights and responsibilities

12.3.1　The question of the compatibility of the Children Act 1989 with the Human Rights Act is really outside the scope of this work. Nevertheless, as schools are frequently faced with dealing with marriage breakdowns, parental disputes and child care cases, it is perhaps worth briefly considering these areas of school work.

12.
PARENTS'
RIGHTS

12.3.2　Fortunately, in general, the Children Act has not been unduly affected by the coming into force of the Human Rights Act. Consequently, the provisions dealing with the rights and entitlements of parents, the meaning of parental responsibility and the availability of care proceedings are as they always have been.

12.3.3 Initially, it was thought that care proceedings in particular would raise issues over Article 8 – the respect for private and family life – as by their very nature, care proceedings interfere with such life. However, Article 8 is a qualified right and, consequently, provided that social service authorities act in accordance with the domestic law, objectively and on sound grounds, the courts are willing to say that the interference with the family's rights is outweighed by the need to protect the interests of the child [see *W & B (Children) and W (Children)* [2001] EWCA Civ 757 and *C v Bury MBC* [2002] EWHC 1438 (Fam)].

13.   Pupils' Rights and Welfare

13.1   Introduction

13.1.1   For all the advances in children's rights since the 1989 Children Act, the rights of the child in educational terms have lagged substantially behind. Indeed, English and Welsh law has treated children very much as the 'property' of their parents, providing their parents with the ability to state preferences, make representations and appeal against decisions affecting their children. The children themselves have, until recently, been able to do very little. In most cases, parents will do the right thing for their children; the problem is where parents do not do so, either because of inactivity or over-activity, either of which have a negative effect on their children's education.

13.1.2   Does this emphasis on the rights and powers of parents at the expense of the children raise any Human Rights Act issues? If the Scottish Government is to be believed, it may do. In s 1 of the Standards in Scotland's Schools etc Act 2000, a statutory right in favour of every child to have a 'school education' is set out. The Explanatory Note to that Act states that 'The establishment of the statutory right to education reflects in the domestic law of Scotland the right to education which is enshrined in the European Convention on Human Rights and in the UN Convention on the Rights of the Child, the United Kingdom being a signatory to these two instruments'. By adding this provision to what was previously equivalent legislation to that in England and Wales, it does suggest that the Scottish Parliament felt that education legislation which did not give express rights to the child would be incompatible with Article 2 of the First Protocol.

13.2   Children's rights

13.2.1   Section 2 of the Standards in Scotland's Schools etc Act 2000 also adopts wording from Article 29(1)(a) of the UN Convention on the Rights of the Child, with the aim of making the development of the personality and talents of the child or young person central to the direction of school education. The provision was designed to put Scottish education authorities under a statutory duty to look beyond general provision to the development of the individual child. Authorities are also required, in carrying out their duty under this provision, to take account of the child's views when making decisions that would significantly affect them: 'In carrying out their duty under this section, an education authority shall have due regard, so far as is reasonably practicable, to the views (if there is a wish to express them) of the child or young person in decisions that significantly affect that child or young person, taking account of the child or young person's age and maturity.' [s 2(2) Standards in Scotland's Schools etc Act 2000]

13.2.2 Whether this provision was strictly necessary to meet Scotland's obligations under the Convention is debatable. Certainly, no case before the ECtHR has raised questions about the lack of 'say' children have in English and Welsh law. Again, perhaps the assumption has been that parents will act in the interests of their children and that their interests will be mutual rather than conflicting.

13.2.3 If Article 2 of the First Protocol does have implications for the wording of UK legislation in 'favour' of parents, steps have already been taken to increase the involvement of children. For example, in the SEN context, the Code of Practice on SEN requires a greater involvement of the child in both the assessment process and the production of individual education plans [Code of Practice on SEN Chapter 3] and the views of the child are given greater prominence in any appeal to the SENDIST [Regulations 13(2)(e) and 30(7) Special Educational Needs Regulations 2001].

13.2.4 Duties may also be imposed on LEAs and governing bodies of maintained schools to have regard to any guidance given by the Secretary of State or the National Assembly for Wales about consultation with pupils in connection with the taking of decisions affecting them [s 176 Education Act 2002]. This is clearly not as strong an obligation as under the Scottish Act and does not have any effect anyway unless the Secretary of State does issue guidance. Nonetheless, it may provide the Secretary of State with the flexibility to issue guidance should the historic preference (based largely, it has to be said, on the historic legal incapacity of minors) for parental rights in education, as opposed to children's rights to education, ever come under threat.

13. PUPILS' RIGHTS AND WELFARE

13.3   The integrity of the child

13.3.1 As we have seen [see Chapter 4], the Convention protects the physical integrity of the individual within both the aegis of Articles 2 and 3, the right to life and protection from inhuman and degrading treatment – but also in respect of Article 8 – the right to have one's private and family life respected.

13.3.2 This could have two effects. In this context, we have already considered [see 8.6*ff* above] what duties may be imposed on LEAs and schools in connection with bullying. Similar requirements will also require public authorities to act positively and proactively to protect children from abuse.

13.3.3 This latter obligation has been recognised, after concerns were expressed about the way some schools had dealt with allegations of child abuse from pupils, in a new provision in the Education Act 2002. Thus, LEAs and governing bodies must both make arrangements for ensuring that their functions are exercised with a view to safeguarding and promoting the welfare of children and children who are pupils at the governing body's school [s 170(1) and (2) Education Act 2002].

13.3.4 Other fundamental provisions to protect the child and secure his or her receipt of suitable education have been considered in Chapter 7 in respect of school attendance.

13.4 Juvenile employment

13.4.1 A more historic desire to protect children has been in force since 1933 and in specific fields even earlier in the context of juvenile employment. This legislation reflects, and continues to do so into the twenty-first century, the desire of early twentieth century legislators to protect children from forced labour, working in heavy industries at all hours and without adequate safety protection. In fact, these provisions preceded whatever the Convention may have laid down in this area.

13.4.2 Article 4 is probably the most relevant Convention Right here, combined with ensuring that a child is not deprived of their right to education under Article 2 of the First Protocol by being forced to work when they should be receiving education.

13.4.3 Article 4 – the prohibition of slavery and forced labour – would deal with the extreme types of juvenile employment which, hopefully, rarely occur in this country, but which might include sweat shop labour.

13.4.4 The important point here is that LEAs will be under a duty to take positive steps to ensure that children for whom they are responsible are not subjected to this type of coercive work. If children were to suffer such indignities and the LEA had done nothing to use its enforcement powers under the Children Act 1972, Children and Young Persons Act 1933 or the other specific pieces of legislation to prevent it, the child might have a claim under the Human Rights Act against the LEA.

13.4.5   In less extreme cases, Article 8 rights, combined with rights under Article 2 of the First Protocol, might come into play if children were in employment which interfered with their private and family life, including their school life and/or they missed out on education because they were required to work during school hours. Again, the national legislation probably ensures that the powers are in place to prevent such employment. The danger will be if LEAs fail to take the necessary enforcement action and a child suffers as a consequence. As with attendance, the fact that the child was happy to go along with the work or it was the parent who employed the child is unlikely to assist an LEA which fails to act.

13.4.6   If enforcement action is taken, there should be few Human Rights Act issues which prevent guilty employers being inspected and prosecuted. There is perhaps a genuine criticism of the law in this area in that it is found in many Acts of Parliament and much of the detail is delegated to local bye-laws so that it is difficult for anyone to know the actual conditions or requirements in a particular area. Nonetheless, it does provide the LEA with the power to require an employer to produce information and to enter premises [s 28 Children and Young Persons Act 1933]. That should mean that no employer could assert Article 8 rights in response to an LEA wishing to check whether he or she is employing children illegally. As opposed to the problem with inspecting home education [considered at 9.9ff above], whilst the arrival of the juvenile employment officer at a factory or office might *prima facie* be an interference with the employer's Article 8 right to respect for his or her private and family life (which does include his or her business), such interference will be in accordance with the law and should be justifiable on the grounds that it is necessary in a democratic society in the interests of public safety, the prevention of crime, the protection of health and possibly morals and the protection of the rights and freedoms of others, i.e. the children.

13.5   Access to records

13.5.1   This topic is considered finally at the end of this section on pupil rights because there can be some confusion over the respective law governing the accumulation of pupil records, their disclosure, data protection, freedom of information and the impact on all these of the Human Rights Act.

13.5.2   Schools, and to a lesser extent LEAs, keep and maintain records in respect of all pupils. In schools this is within the ambit of the Education (Pupil Information) (England) Regulations 2000 [SI 2000/297], the Data Protection Act 1998 and the Data Protection (Subject Access

Modification) (Education) Order 2000 [SI 2000/414]. By their nature such records are very private and often contain sensitive information about family backgrounds. Disclosure of these records is therefore carefully regulated by the education specific regulations and the Data Protection Act. But will this regulation be sufficient and will the Human Rights Act add anything more?

13.5.3 Arguably, now that the Human Rights Act is in force, schools would be ill-advised to rely on the domestic regulations and assume that if they disclose information in accordance with their provisions they will be safe from challenge. The reason is that whilst most disclosure will be permissible, the Human Rights Act and Article 8 in particular may impose an additional layer of responsibility. This is because Article 8 first of all requires public authorities to respect a person's private and family life. The communication of sensitive information held by a public body is *prima facie* an interference with that right. Article 8 is a qualified right and as such the action can be justified but only if it meets the qualifications in *the* Article; the fact it may meet the qualifications in the domestic legislation and regulations may not be good enough. Ensuring that disclosure is in accordance with the regulations merely means that the first qualification in Article 8(2) is met, i.e. that the interference with the right is in accordance with the law. What a school would have to do, and this goes beyond the scope of the domestic law (hence why it is said that relying just on that may not be good enough), is to satisfy itself that the disclosure is necessary in a democratic society in the interests of one of the matters listed in Article 8(2) and that the interference with the right was proportionate. In most cases, those criteria will be met and the information disclosed as before, but those who disclose such information may in future have to be sure that if challenged they can demonstrate that they have considered each and every point under Article 8 before disclosing the record.

13.5.4 Having examined parent and pupil rights, we will finally turn to school staff and consider what (if any) rights they may have under the Human Rights Act.

13.
PUPILS' RIGHTS
AND WELFARE

14. Staffing

14.1 Introduction

14.1.1 In many respects the issues of staffing under the Human Rights Act are potentially so significant and extensive that a work of this nature can hardly do justice to the subject. Readers who wish to obtain in-depth and detailed guidance on the employment aspects of the Human Rights Act should therefore consult one of the specific works on the subject.

14.1.2 Nevertheless, there may be some aspects of the general employment law effect of the Human Rights Act which will have particular pertinence for LEA and school staff and these will be considered in this chapter.

14.1.3 For this purpose, it is assumed that in their capacity as employers, schools and LEAs are, in fact, public authorities for the purposes of the Human Rights Act. As has been considered at length [see 3.7.3*ff* above] that is by no means certain as the private law nature of the relationship could mean that they fall within s 6(5) of the Human Rights Act and are therefore not matters with which a public authority, as such, is involved.

14.2 Freedom of expression

14.2.1 When the Human Rights Act first came into effect, concerns were expressed that it would permit staff to dress as they liked and say what they liked, all in the interest of their freedom of expression [under Article 10]. In fact, the apocryphal anticipation has been rendered somewhat redundant because, by and large, teachers are sensible people.

14.2.2 Similarly, employers have, by and large, shown good sense and not taken action against staff for expressing legitimate opinions.

14.2.3 The truth is also that domestic law has already put in place protections to assist employers as much as possible in meeting Human Rights Act obligations or, if they do not, providing effective remedies in the domestic tribunals, without the need for anyone to assert a Convention Right. Examples include the long history of anti-discrimination law updated as required by European Community and Union, not Convention, law and more recent legislation to protect whistleblowers [see the Public Interest Disclosure Act 1998].

14.2.4 Freedom of expression could, nonetheless, still be an issue and employers need to tread warily. If they were to take action against what had been an expressed view falling within Article 10, that action could only be justified if it met the qualifications to that Article, i.e. the restrictions are prescribed by law and are necessary in a democratic society for the listed reasons and are proportionate. Get that wrong and the employer will be in breach. As an illustration, in *Vogt v Federal Republic of Germany* [(1995) Series A No 323 21 EHRR 205], the ECtHR held that the dismissal of a teacher because of her membership of the German Communist Party was a breach of Article 10.

14.2.5 Similar issues arise under Article 9 with regard to freedom of thought, conscience and religion. Certain expression of such views must be tolerated by an employer, but it is not necessary for either the employer or other employees to tolerate racist or sexist views or other opinions which are not acceptable in a democratic society etc. Holding such views, though, as opposed to expressing them, would probably be a different matter.

14.2.6 Employers should also respect their employee's religion by making reasonable allowances, for example, by permitting Muslim employees time off where possible for daily prayers or perhaps the provision of a quiet place for such prayers. In any event, most Article 9 issues are likely to be covered by the Race Relations Act 1976.

14.3 Dealing with staff

14.3.1 It goes without saying that employees wherever and whenever employed should be treated fairly and their religious and political opinions given due respect as outlined above. One aspect of the Convention which is not usually considered to be relevant in the employment sphere is Article 8, the right to respect for private and family life.

14.3.2 In fact, an employer may fall foul of Article 8 both in terms of the direct impact of his or her actions (a person's work or business may fall within their private or family life and their office within their home [see, for example, *Halford v United Kingdom* (1997) 24 EHRR 523]), as well as the indirect effect of what he or she does during work hours on his or her employee's behaviour and relationships outside of work.

14.
STAFFING

14.3.3 In the former case, monitoring of an employee's work is not considered to infringe Article 8. Much interest has however been expressed about an employer's ability to monitor e-mails and the employee's use of the internet. This is probably particularly pertinent to staff who use school computers to which children may have access.

14.3.4 It would appear that such action can be justified (by analogy with the ECtHR's decision in *X v Commission of the European Communities* [[1995] IRLR 320] concerning compulsory HIV testing) as follows. There will be no breach of Article 8 if the employee consents, hence the need to make clear that an employer will be monitoring an employee's e-mails in advance; consent will then be assumed. Surreptitious monitoring will conversely probably amount to a breach. If the monitoring is necessary and proportionate in the circumstances of the employment, then such monitoring may well be permissible.

14.3.5 The disclosure of allegations of child abuse relating to an employee may also be permissible provided there was a pressing need for the disclosure of such information and, in balancing the need to protect children against the right of an individual to a private life, the body making the disclosure had to consider a) its belief in the truth of the allegations, b) the interest of the third party in obtaining the information, and c) the degree of risk posed by the individual if the disclosure was not made [*R v A Police Authority in the Midlands and A County Council in the Midlands ex p LM* (2000) COD 41, (2000) 1 FLR 612].

14.4 Workplace bullying

14.4.1 Workplace bullying may also infringe a number of Convention Rights and, as with protecting children from bullying, the employer has an obligation both not to commit such acts himself but also to take steps to protect an employee from such action committed by others.

14.4.2 Normally, such bullying could amount to an infringement of Article 3 – freedom from inhuman or degrading treatment. This does require quite serious mistreatment beyond the pressures normally associated with a particular job, but in such severe cases, some of which have recently been reported in the press [see, for example, *Teacher wins stress payout of £100,000, The Independent*, 9 March 2001], it would not be fanciful to suggest that an employee could have a claim under the Human Rights Act as well as such other legislation as may found a cause of action under existing domestic law. Schools should also ensure that members of staff are not subjected to bullying by pupils, as well as managers and fellow members of staff [see, for example, some *obiter* comments in *Pearce v Governing Body of Mayfield School* [2001] EWCA Civ 1347].

14.4.3 The pressures do have to be severe. Thus an Ofsted inspection *per se* will not suffice, although if either the inspectors or the head teacher subjected staff to humiliation or other degrading treatment, Article 3 might kick into play.

14.
STAFFING

14.4.4 Article 4 – the prohibition of forced labour: however much a member of staff of a public authority feels they are in slavery or servitude, is unlikely to be invoked as again this requires a very high level of compulsion, almost akin to keeping an employee in captivity.

14.5 Disciplinary appeals

14.5.1 Whilst we have considered that most panels and tribunals relating to pupils do not fall within Article 6 – the right to a fair trial – because they do not involve the determination of a person's civil rights, the same will not be true of a decision and appeal in respect of a member of staff's dismissal. Quite clearly, determining a persons' contract of employment will be a determination of a civil right (subject to the proviso set out in 14.1.3 and 3.7.3*ff* that the employer is in fact a public authority for these purposes).

14.5.2 Consequently, Article 6 will apply in respect of the fairness of the entire disciplinary process. (There is an argument that as an appeal could be brought to an Employment Tribunal, that would provide sufficient protection not to require an employer to comply with Article 6 in its procedures, but that could be a mistaken view and, indeed, would probably now put the employer in breach of domestic law requirements in respect of fair and unfair dismissals). However, the provisions contained in domestic law, currently in Schedules 16 and 17 of SSFA 1998 [to be replaced by regulations under ss 35 and 36 Education Act 2002] provide a process which should be Human Rights Act compliant. Again, it is probable that the Human Rights Act adds little to the requirements imposed on a disciplinary process by domestic law, including the principles of natural justice.

14.6 Discrimination

14.6.1 Again, Article 14 could well apply when combined with the exercise of another Convention Right to prohibit discrimination in the employment field. In fact, given the breadth of existing domestic anti-discrimination legislation, the Human Rights Act is likely to have little impact, especially when the new European Discrimination Directive becomes operative, requiring the UK Government to prohibit forms of discrimination beyond the race, sex and disability discrimination currently prohibited.

14.6.2 Until that Directive takes effect, however, allegations about forms of discrimination which are not currently prohibited by domestic law may well be made under the Human Rights Act. This was the main thrust of

14.
STAFFING

the claimant's case in *Pearce* in trying to establish that the Human Rights Act meant that sexual orientation discrimination was already prohibited. Ageism may be another form of discrimination which will be challenged by use of the Human Rights Act, although in all cases it must be remembered that Article 14 is not a stand alone Convention Right but only applies in relation to the exercise of other rights.

14.6.3 As stated at the start of this section, there are many potential issues in the area of employment which may be affected by the Human Rights Act. Here we have just identified a few areas which leap immediately to mind; there may be many others, or, as is possible with a large part of the Human Rights Act, there may be many other possible areas of infringement, but whether in practice challenges will be successful is debatable. Again, as with all aspects of the Act since it came into force, LEAs and schools should feel reassured that the pessimists who feared a grinding halt to public sector activity have so far been proved wrong.

14.
STAFFING

15. Conclusion

15.1 Concluding remarks and some predictions

15.1.1 This book has charted a strange course. It started with an examination of the fundamental reasons behind the original European Convention on Human Rights – an end to death squads, concentration camps and forced labour – and ended up with an analysis of the issue of a school teacher's ability to speak his or her mind or ignore dress codes. There is perhaps the impression that, as T.S. Eliot might say, we have ended not with a bang but a whimper.

15.1.2 Perhaps that is, in some respects, intentional. This work was designed to inform and reassure. What hopefully becomes evident is that the Human Rights Act has to date had an impact, quite properly, on substantial issues, but has not, so far, had a significant impact on the everyday work of schools and LEAs. The predictions of doom and gloom have proved unfounded and the fact that we have been reduced to searching for potential infringements among the minutiae of LEA work does, perhaps, illustrate why public sector employees should not be unduly worried by the effect the Human Rights Act has had or may have on their work.

15.1.3 This is not by any means, however, an endorsement of complacency; as has been seen, attempts have been made to invoke the Human Rights Act in the education field and, there is no doubt, efforts will continue to be made in the future. A sensible, proportionate response is to be prepared, to ensure procedures are compliant with both national law and the additional burdens of the Human Rights Act, and to act reasonably and properly when making decisions; just ignoring the Act, and hoping it will never affect you, is a sure fire way of ensuring that a challenge will be made and may be successful.

15.1.4 Throughout this book, we have tried to address potential areas of education work, which may have human rights elements. In some cases, the reassurance has been that most aspects of our work do not raise human rights issues in the first place; in others, the courts have provided the reassurance by dismissing claims which invoke the 1998 Act. There are, however, some areas where the law is still uncertain, principally because they have not been tested in the courts. So, as a conclusion to this work, it is perhaps helpful to try

15.
CONCLUSION

to identify areas where court challenges are currently pending or to offer some predictions on areas of education work against which challenges may arise in the future.

15.2 Detention

15.2.1 Detention has always been a contentious issue between schools and parents. As schools complain that their other methods of discipline are being eroded, it would be unfortunate if this particular punishment was to be removed or unduly restricted. As explained above [see 8.3], it is hoped that the statutory conditions in s 550B of the EA 1996 will enable the courts to uphold the legality of the punishment.

15.2.2 However, this outcome is by no means certain. In Scotland [see *Classrooms ban detention after pupil cites human rights*, *The Independent*, 7 January 2003] education authorities have already warned schools to drop detentions as a result of a legal challenge being brought by a pupil at Speyside High School in Banffshire. Freya Macdonald's claim against Moray Council is that an after-school detention she received 'seriously disrupted her education and violated her human rights'. Her lawyers are apparently arguing that such a detention contravened Article 5 on the basis it is illegal to detain children without a court order, and Article 2 of the First Protocol; and, for good measure, that it amounted to degrading treatment contrary to Article 3 (prohibition on inhuman or degrading treatment).

15.2.3 The comment might be made, if reverting to the point made at the start of this chapter, that keeping a teenager behind after school for an hour or half an hour is hardly the same as imprisonment without trial or state sanctioned torture, which those articles were originally drafted to prevent. Nevertheless, a number of Scottish education authorities do appear to have taken the action seriously and have warned schools against imposing detentions. Other Scottish education authorities have declared that detentions should not be imposed without parental permission. This, however, would seem merely to return us to the old problem that existed before s 550B was introduced: namely, that schools would find it difficult, if not impossible, to discipline the children of un-cooperative parents, otherwise than resorting to the more draconian punishment of exclusion.

15.2.4 If detention were to be held unlawful, schools would, it seems to follow, be forced to exclude pupils for relative minor offences; how else could those children be properly disciplined? Here there is therefore the potential for the irony that whilst exclusion is permissible [see *Sulak v*

15.
CONCLUSION

Turkey 84-A DR 98 (1996)] under the Human Rights Act, the lesser punishment of detention would not be. That does not make much sense.

15.2.5 It is to be regretted that the authorities in Scotland have reacted in this way – over-reacted in the author's view. The author may be proved wrong, but the existing case law (and particularly the decision in *Family TV v Austria* [64 DR 176 (1989)]) would suggest that punitive detention is permissible against children provided that it does not involve any restriction on liberty greater than that imposed as a normal incident of bringing up children. So long, therefore, as parents are not prevented from keeping their children in, grounding them or whatever phrase enjoys current usage, it is suggested that a school will not be acting unlawfully if it imposes similar punishments. And provided, of course, that in imposing a detention, the school complies with the national law and, in particular, the conditions laid down in s 550B of the EA 1996.

15.3 Religious tolerance, religious and philosophical convictions

15.3.1 The subject of religious tolerance is both topical and probably, in the context of this book, one of the more important issues which may affect schools and LEAs. The Stephen Lawrence Inquiry and the Race Relations (Amendment) Act have highlighted the importance of race relations and respect for different races, but the Human Rights Act may act as a spur for securing greater tolerance of others' views and protecting the rights of particular groups.

15.3.2 The Government may be taking steps to bring religious discrimination and intolerance into the same category of protection as race discrimination, but before it does so, the Human Rights Act may provide a degree of both freedom and reassurance for members of minority faiths. Already, in *R (on the application of K) v Newham LBC* [[2002] EWHC 405 (Admin)] the courts have asserted that recognition must be given to the religious beliefs of parents where admissions authorities are making decisions as to school places. This may be developed further. Already, one LEA, Portsmouth [*Information for Parents – Admission to Primary and Secondary Schools 2003-2004* Portsmouth City Council], has amended its admissions policy to provide that the first priority in the event of oversubscription for places in a community school is that ' the parent has expressed a religious and philosophical conviction for their child to attend that school'. It is suggested that such a change is not required as a consequence of *K v Newham* (that case merely making clear that an admission authority had to enable parents to express their convictions and once they had done

15.
CONCLUSION

so, had to respect them) nor is it perhaps the most sensible of policies. As we have seen, defining religious and philosophical convictions has exercised the ECtHR and there is no certainty as to what can or cannot be considered as such a conviction. Pity then the poor admission officer or admission appeal panel required to make a judgement as to whether a parent is expressing a conviction, whether it is religious or philosophical and what effect it will have in any event on their decision, especially, say, at Key Stage 1.

15.3.3 The point becomes even more contentious when the question of faith schools and denominational education is raised. Respect for religious beliefs is clearly supported by the plurality of schools available within England and Wales. But what though of the non-religious, the atheist or the agnostic? In a thought-provoking article [*Must we believe in God to get a good school?, The Independent*, 9 January 2003] Caroline Haydon described the difficulties in securing secondary education for her son, when the schools closest to her home were denominational schools. Was it discrimination, she asked, that, because her family were not members of the schools' particular faiths, her son had less chance of securing a place at local schools? The answer is probably yes. Why is it, that in an age when society is becoming increasingly secular [in *The Independent* article referred to above, the National Secular Society is quoted as saying that more than 30 per cent of people disbelieve in God, compared to 2 per cent in the 1940s], the education system continues to maintain a degree of religious discrimination and favouritism? Is this, though, a human rights issue?

15.3.4 The answer here is probably not. Certainly, however tempting it might be to some, the Human Rights Act could not be used to mount a challenge to the whole system of denominational education. As has been seen, the European Convention on Human Rights was, in this regard, designed to ensure plurality of religion and to protect the expression of beliefs. It could not be used to compel a state to provide schools teaching a particular curriculum or in a particular language [*The Belgian Linguistics Case*], provided that the state did not prevent parents educating their children in particular ways if they wished and within reason. So, equally, it is unlikely to be available to assist those who wish to create a wholly secular education system and take religion out of schools.

15.3.5 What about the parent in the similar situation to the parent in *The Independent* article? If the educational provision prevented a parent having their child educated in accordance with their religious views, there might be a breach. What then if the effect of school organisation in a particular area is to prevent parents who do not believe in or belong

15.
CONCLUSION

to the religions of denominational schools in their area from securing equal treatment in the allocation of places? Sadly, there is probably not a lot that they can do, however unfair the situation may appear to be. Discrimination, in itself, is not unlawful under the Human Rights Act; such parents would therefore have to try to point to infringement of other Convention Rights, either alone or in combination with such perceived discrimination. So long as there are places available in non-denominational schools, within a reasonable travelling distance, however, it is unlikely that parents in such a situation will be able to establish a claim.

15.3.6 Nonetheless, this whole area of religious freedom, expression and tolerance has the potential to create some interesting Human Rights Act cases in the future.

15.4 Sexual orientation discrimination

15.4.1 On a related subject, another area where the Human Rights Act may have an impact is in the context of discrimination on the grounds of sexual orientation. In a sense, the human rights aspect of this is academic as the Government will have to make such action unlawful to meet its obligations under European law.

15.4.2 Nonetheless, at the time of finalising this guide, the matter is under consideration by the House of Lords in the context of a claim that abuse meted out to a lesbian teacher by school pupils is unlawful discrimination as a consequence of the Human Rights Act [see the case of *Pearce v Governing Body of Mayfield School* [2001] EWCA Civ 1347 for the decision appealed against].

15.4.3 Perhaps here, the Human Rights Act might achieve a degree of fairness for all groups in society otherwise lacking in national law at the moment.

15.5 Non-attendance – prosecutions

15.5.1 This is an area where, as we have seen [Chapter 7 above], there may be a conflict between the effect of the Human Rights Act and the Government's aim to crack down on truancy. Although the High Court in *Barnfather v Islington LBC and Secretary of State for Education and Skills* [[2003] EWHC 418 (Admin)] has for the time being decided that the provisions allowing parents to be prosecuted for their children's non-attendance do not infringe Article 6, there are still questions over the strict liability nature of the offence. These questions remain, in part,

15.
CONCLUSION

still outstanding because of the contrary position taken in the Scottish courts in *O'Hagan v Rea* [2001] SLT (Sh Ct) 30 and 7.2 above. The courts may not therefore have seen the last of such challenges.

15.5.2 There are a number of ways, however, to avoid a situation in which the aim of reducing truancy can be undermined by a Human Rights Act challenge. First, and perhaps most importantly, LEAs should exercise a degree of common sense when deciding whether to prosecute a parent. Thus, they should be very cautious of taking criminal action against a parent who, though strictly liable under s 444(1) of the EA 1996, has no control over their child's attendance, the most obvious example being the separated parent who no longer lives in the family home. But this would also include the parent who for physical reasons is simply unable to secure their child's attendance, however much they may try to get them to school.

15.5.3 If that still does not make prosecutions safe from challenge, then the second option will be for the Government to amend the legislation and convert the offence into one where a parent's intent or recklessness in failing to secure their child's attendance should be relevant; in effect, the offence will have to cease to be one of strict liability. To a certain extent, that has been done by creating the more serious offence in s 444(1A) and may, now, in light of *Barnfather*, be unnecessary in terms of the 'lesser' s 444(1) offence.

15.6 Exclusion appeals

15.6.1 Exclusion is, more probably than not [see Chapter 8 and *Sulak v Turkey*], lawful under the Human Rights Act. To date, the courts have also accepted that the appeal arrangements which enable parents or pupils to appeal against decisions to exclude are also human rights compatible, provided a number of safeguards remain in place [see *S, T, P v Brent LBC, Oxfordshire County Council, Head Teacher of Elliott School, the Secretary of State for Education and Skills and Others* [[2002] EWCA Civ 693].

15.6.2 But the Court of Appeal has given warning [see comments of Schiemann LJ in *S, T, P v Brent LBC, Oxfordshire County Council, Head Teacher of Elliott School, the Secretary of State for Education and Skills and Others* [2002] EWCA Civ 693] that they may want to revisit the protections available to excluded pupils in the future. The Court also appeared unhappy at the reliance which has been placed on the decision in *Simpson v United Kingdom* [64 DR 188 (1989)], in which the Commission decided that a place at a school was not a 'civil right' as such and that, consequently, Article 6 – the right to a fair trial – did not apply to any decision or appeals relating to placement at school. The *Simpson* decision has always seemed dubious. Though probably correct in terms of a strict interpretation of the meaning of a 'civil right' under the Convention, it is difficult to reconcile with the increasing emphasis on a parent's or pupil's 'rights' in national law [for example, the right, in principle, to seek compensation for negligent education – see *X v Bedfordshire County Council* and *Phelps v Hillingdon LBC*]. If a court in the future decides to distance itself or find a way of avoiding the decision in *Simpson* (and the warnings are there in *S,T,P*), the appeal system currently in place to deal with permanent exclusions (and also the admission appeal process) may be under threat. Administratively and organisationally difficult though it may be, the Human Rights Act might eventually encourage the creation of a new style Education Tribunal independent from the interests of the schools and LEAs whose decisions are under challenge.

15.7 Rights of children

15.7.1 Education law is very much centred on the rights, entitlements and preferences of parents. Children are reliant on their parents stating a preference for them to attend a school which will be the best for them, for ensuring that they attend school and for protecting their special educational needs. There is no problem where parents act scrupulously in their children's interests, but what if they do not?

15.7.2 Currently, there is little that the child can do him or herself to protect their education. They cannot appeal against a decision to refuse them a place at school; they cannot, whilst under 16, appeal against a decision to exclude them from school; nor can they appeal against decisions relating to their special educational needs.

15.7.3 The voice of children may achieve greater effect as a result of s 176 of the Education Act 2002 (the duty imposed on governing bodies and LEAs to have regard to guidance issued by the Secretary of State to ensure consultation with children in relation to matters affecting them) but, nonetheless, the majority of education 'rights' can be enforced only by adults.

15.7.4 Will the Human Rights Act have an impact on this? The UN Convention on the Rights of the Child certainly sought to give priority to pupils' views in respect of their school education, and the Standards in Scotland's Schools etc Act 2000 was probably influenced by the European Convention on Human Rights when placing an obligation on education authorities to have regard to the views of children when making decisions that substantially affect them [see for more detail Chapter 13 above].

15.7.5 It is conceivable that this does not go far enough and that there may be a case where our law's willingness to subjugate the 'rights' of children to those of their parents may amount to an infringement of a stand-alone Convention Right and could, in conjunction with the exercise of such rights, amount to discrimination under Article 14.

15.7.6 Such a case may be some way off, but if incorporation of the European Convention into United Kingdom law is to have some true and substantial effect, as opposed to the trivial so beloved of the tabloids, it would be no bad thing if it were to achieve greater rights for children within the education system.

15.8 Beware complacency

15.8.1 Human rights law is fascinating and interesting because of its context, its history and the important issues to society which it affects. It may be less fascinating and interesting to those who have to work their way though the difficulties it may create in LEAs or schools. Nonetheless, human rights have, as the Government proclaimed, 'Come Home' and they will feature as a core aspect of all public authority work in the future. What is important, and where hopefully this book will assist, is in ensuring that a proper perspective is kept on the 1998 Act's effect; do not overreact but equally do not treat it lightly or as an inconvenience to administration

15.
CONCLUSION

Abbreviations

(Including published law reports and the new form of neutral citation)

the 1998 Act	Human Rights Act 1998
AC	Law Reports: Appeal Cases
All ER	All England Law Reports
All ER (D)	All England Law Reports (Digest)
Article 2 of the First Protocol	Article 2 of the First Protocol to the Convention – The Right to Education
BHRC	Butterworths Human Rights Cases
CA	Court of Appeal
COD	Crown Office Digest
The Commission	The European Commission of Human Rights
The Committee of Ministers	The Committee of Ministers of the Council of Europe
The Convention	The European Convention for the Protection of Human Rights and Fundamental Freedoms
DR	Council of Europe. European Commission on Human Rights. Decisions & Reports
EA 1996	Education Act 1996
ECtHR	The European Court of Human Rights
EdCR	Education Case Reports
EHHR	European Human Rights Reports
EHRLR	European Human Rights Law Review
ELR	Education Law Reports
EPLI	Education, Public Law and the Individual (Hart Publishing)
EMIE	Education Management Information Exchange
EWCA Civ	England and Wales Court of Appeal Civil Division – Neutral Case Citation
EWHC	England and Wales High Court – Neutral Case Citation
FCR	Family Court Reporter
FLR	Family Law Reports
HL	House of Lords
HRLR	Human Rights Law Reports
Human Rights Act	Human Rights Act 1998
ICR	Industrial Case Reports
IRLR	Industrial Relations Law Reports

KB	Law Reports: King's Bench Division
LEA	Local education authority
LGR	Local Government Reports
LS Gaz R	Law Society Gazette reports
QB	Law Reports: Queen's Bench Division
SLT	Scottish law Times
ScotHC	High Court of Scotland – Neutral Case Citation
SEN	Special educational needs
SEND	Special Educational Needs and Disability Act
SENDIST	Special Educational Needs and Disability Tribunal
SENT	Special Educational Needs Tribunal
SOC	School Organisation Committee
Sol Jo	Solicitors Journal
SSFA 1998	School Standards and Framework Act 1999
UKHL	United Kingdom House of Lords – Neutral Case Citation
WLR	Weekly Law Reports
YB	Year Book of the European Commission of Human Rights

Index